Cognition
and Curriculum
Reconsidered

SECOND EDITION

ELLIOT W. EISNER

**TEACHERS
COLLEGE
PRESS**

Teachers College, Columbia University
New York and London

Published by Teachers College Press, 1234 Amsterdam Avenue
New York, NY 10027

Library of Congress Cataloging-in-Publication Data

Eisner, Elliot W.
    Cognition and curriculum reconsidered / Elliot W. Eisner — 2nd
ed.
        p.   cm.
    Rev. ed. of: Cognition and curriculum. c1982.
    Includes bibliographical references (p.   ) and index.
    ISBN 0-8077-3311-3 (acid-free paper). — ISBN 0-8077-3310-5 (pbk.:
acid-free paper)
    1. Cognitive learning—United States.   2. Curriculum planning—
United States.   3. Literacy—United States.   I. Eisner, Elliot W.
Cognition and curriculum.   II. Title.
LB1590.3.E37   1994
370.15′2—dc20   94-320

Printed on acid-free paper

Manufactured in the United States of America

01 00 99 98 97 96 95 94   8 7 6 5 4 3 2 1

Cognition
and Curriculum
Reconsidered

I believe that the individual who is to be educated is a social individual, and that society is an organic union of individuals. If we eliminate the social factor from the child we are left only with an abstraction; if we eliminate the individual factor from society, we are left only with an inert and lifeless mass. Education, therefore, must begin with a psychological insight into the child's capacities, interests, and habits. It must be controlled at every point by reference to these same considerations. These powers, interests, and habits must be continually interpreted—we must know what they mean. They must be translated into terms of their social equivalents—into terms of what they are capable of in the way of social service.

John Dewey
My Pedagogic Creed, 1897

Contents

Preface

This book is about the relationship among sensation, conception, and representation. Its thesis is seductively straightforward: the senses are our primary information pickup systems and provide the content through which our conceptual life takes form. It argues further that the concepts that constitute our conceptual life are images formed within the ''material'' that each of the senses provides, either singly or in combination with the content of other senses. Concepts precede their linguistic transformation. I argue that language serves as one of the ways through which our conceptual life is made public. Further, I believe that the representation of that life must itself employ a form of representation that is made of material available to our sensory capacities; thus forms of representation may appeal primarily to our senses of sight, touch, sound, smell, and taste. Finally, the types of meaning that we are able to construe from the forms of representation we encounter are related both to the limits and possibilities of those forms and to our ability to ''read'' them. Forms of representation both reveal and conceal. They make particular kinds of meanings possible. They give us access to unique worlds.

This view of the sources of the content of our mental life is not one that has been popular in the Western world. Mind, according to Plato, is most acutely and dependably realized when it transcends the sensibilities: humans are most rational when the empirical world, the world that Plato believed to be fugitive and undependable, is relinquished for the world of pure reason; for Plato, the senses got in the way. Plato was not alone in this view. Descartes also promoted a view of mind that in its finest moments was freed from the constraints of the body. Mathematics represented for him, as dialectics represented for Plato, the quintessence of rational thought. Comprehension of the tidy universe that Enlightenment philosophers believed to exist has remained a pervasive yet tacit aim in contemporary schooling. Abstract thought, the cognitive ideal we embrace, is disembodied.

This book adumbrates another vision. It calls our attention to the importance of the senses as a means through which the qualitative world we all inhabit is experienced. It calls our attention to the importance of perception and the cognitive character that it ineluctably possesses. This vision seeks to acknowledge and honor the role of imagination in the construction of possible worlds. And, most important, it seeks to reveal the contributions that different forms of representation, various modes of treatment, and different syntactical structures make to the meanings we are able to create and experience.

The ability to secure meaning in the course of our experience is a basic human need; we all want to lead meaningful lives. But meaning is not simply found; it is constructed. In a sense the ability to "encode" and "decode" the meanings construed from different forms of representation requires a form of literacy. Not literacy in the literal sense, but literacy in the metaphorical sense. Literacy, as I use the term, is the ability to encode or decode meaning in any of the forms of representation used in the culture to convey or express meaning. In this sense, I believe, one of the major aims of education is the development of multiple forms of literacy. What we ought to develop, in my view, is the student's ability to access meaning within the variety of forms of representation that humans use to represent the contents of their consciousness. These forms are no less important in the fine arts than they are in the sciences; they are no less important in mathematics than they are in the humanities. Further, the provision of opportunities to learn how to use such literacies ought to contribute to greater educational equity for students, especially for those whose aptitudes reside in the use of forms of representation now marginalized by our current educational priorities. Further still, I believe that, at base, the process of education itself has to do with the creation of mind. Mind, unlike brain, which is a biological given, is a form of cultural achievement. Schools are cultures. They are cultures for creating minds. Thus the presence of different forms of representation is a presence that activates, develops, and refines mind. In this sense, those of us in the field of education are in the construction business, and the environments and opportunities we create in our schools enable children, in turn, to create the kinds of minds they wish to own.

This, then, in brief, sketches the line of argument I have developed in this book.

A word about the history of this volume. In 1979, I was invited by the John Dewey Society to give the John Dewey Lecture. That lecture culminated in a book titled *Cognition and Curriculum: A Basis for Deciding What to Teach.* This present volume is a substantial revision of that earlier publication; more than half of the material in that earlier volume has been entirely replaced by new material, and other sections have been partially revised. My hope is that in an era of national goals, national standards, national report cards, national assessment, and national curricula the ideas in this volume will stimulate and support a vision of the possibilities of education other than those that seem intractably premised upon a business-oriented competitive view of schooling and an intellectually narrow conception of mind.

I am perhaps more aware than most of the unfinished nature of the material that I have developed here. The problems that I am coping with are among the most difficult I have encountered as a scholar in the field of education. This volume should, therefore, be seen as a further effort to point toward what I believe to be a promising direction, rather than a water-tight argument or a specific set of procedures for achieving important educational goals. This book has more to do with direction-setting than with the creation of a map displaying a detailed route leading to a specific destination. If the work is successful, it ought to stimulate others to push further than I have been able to travel.

1 Reforming Educational Reform

It is difficult, even for the casual observer of American education, not to conclude that our schools are in a deep state of crisis. All of the media, almost all politicians, and most of the public polls express considerable anxiety about the sorry state of our students' performance. To remedy matters, they search for ways to make them "world class." What exactly "world class" means in the context of educating the young is not altogether clear, although it seems to mean that on international examinations of student performance, especially in math and science, American students will rise from their lowly state near the bottom of the ladder and ascend to the very top. What we cannot seem to do in the American automobile industry, we believe we can do in the education business.

Political Mandates for Change

If you detect a touch of cynicism in the foregoing remarks, your intuition is correct. It seems almost yesterday that we had another educational crisis. It was in 1983 when *A Nation at Risk* (National Commission on Excellence in Education, 1983) was published. Its opening lines read as follows:

> If an unfriendly foreign power had attempted to impose on America the mediocre educational performance that exists today, we might well have viewed it as an act of war. As it stands, we have

1

allowed this to happen to ourselves. We have even squandered the
gains in student achievement made in the wake of the Sputnik
challenge. Moreover, we have dismantled essential support systems which helped make those gains possible. We have, in effect,
been committing an act of unthinking, unilateral educational dis-
armament. (p. 5)

What could be more damning? America has never been invaded
by a foreign army, let alone lost a war (aside from Vietnam), yet
what foreign armies could not do, our schools unhappily are achieving. American schools, *A Nation at Risk* claimed, were destroying
America.[1]

A Nation at Risk was not an unread government document. It
found its way to every major American television network, it was
reported in all of the major newspapers, and it was discussed by
countless school boards throughout the nation. *A Nation at Risk* not
only painted a dismal portrait of our schools, it also suggested remedies to cure them. These remedies resided in an emphasis on "the
five new basics." Now only a few years later, with a level of educational analysis not much deeper than that which appeared in *A Nation
at Risk*, we have its counterpart—*America 2000* (U.S. Department of
Education, 1991). Are current calls for educational reform likely to be
more successful than those we have heard in the past? Will a national
testing program and a public report card do the trick? Is a vision of
education tied to an international race for educational superiority
what we want or need for our children or for this country? Can
schools do more with less money? Are we, at last, on the road to
educational recovery?

Whether the public display of student report cards will make it
possible for schools to become better places for students or teachers
is not entirely clear. Also a mystery is why it is thought that an appropriate cure for educational ills is a common examination for 47
million students attending 108,000 schools overseen by 16,000 school
boards located in fifty states serving a population as diverse as ours.
As for model schools, another of *America 2000*'s recommendations,
American education has not been without them. The difficulty is not
the creation of model schools. The difficulty is the idea that somehow
schools can be "replicated" in other contexts, as if the process was
biological rather than political and social. Furthermore, even the idea
of crisis is not particularly clear in the context of schools. Is there a
crisis in American education for all students or only for some? What
is the nature of this crisis? Is it that too many students in some

segments of our community are dropping out of high school before they graduate? Is this due to the schools' failure, or might there be other causes? Is the crisis one of poor test performance? If so, for whom? Is the crisis due to incompetent teachers, poorly motivated students, parents who do not care enough about their children's education, the escalating incidence of single-parent families, the level of racism in our society, the increasing number of our children growing up in poverty, the inadequacy of prenatal care afforded the poorest among us, the side effects on children of twenty or more hours per week watching television? Do all of these factors contribute to the ways in which our children perform in school? If so, what might *these* factors mean for the improvement of schools?

In many ways, the desire to establish a common set of national educational standards is understandable. It is also understandable that there is a strong desire to use a common test to measure their achievement. Many people in and out of education have lost confidence in the schools' capacity to deliver the educational goods they believe they have paid for. The source of their concerns is often the decline in students' scores on the College Board's Scholastic Aptitude Test (SAT). From 1966 to 1990, the average SAT verbal score dropped 42 points, from 466 to 424. During the same period the average SAT math score dropped 18 points, from 492 to 474 (College Entrance Examination Board, 1989). The drop has been steady. Yet such evidence is hardly adequate for appraising the quality of American schools. The SAT is a multiple choice test having eighty items in each of its two sections: math and verbal. It takes only six missed items to account for a drop from 466 to 424 in the verbal section and only four missed items to explain a drop from 492 to 474 in the math section. My point here is not to provide an apology for dropping test scores, it is simply to provide an indication of the shallow analysis that has gone into the interpretation of the meaning of these scores. What kind of predictive validity do people believe five or six multiple choice items have? And might the drop in SAT scores be, in part, a result of an expanding, more diversified population taking the SATs? Such information is seldom provided to the public. Instead, a drop of two points from one year to the next makes national headlines.

I make these points and raise these questions to complicate the simplistic analyses of schooling that have bombarded the American public over the past decade; to have a good word for schools is virtually to confess having a lack of standards. To introduce what might be called mitigating factors is to take the risk of being seen as an apologist for the ''education establishment.'' We seem to prefer slogans. "Just say no to drugs" finds its counterpart in "First in science and math by the year 2000."

One reason why shallow analyses of schooling are not promising for improving schools is that they typically fail to identify the underlying conditions that make schools what they are. In a very real sense, they address symptoms, and because they neglect the deeper structural conditions that animate schools, the "solutions" that are prescribed provide no actual solution. Using a national examination—the American Achievement Test—to take the educational temperature of schools and then to publicize the temperature is likely to be as useful for curing the ills of schools as taking a patient's temperature and publicizing its magnitude would be for curing the patient. Temperature taking in education will, at best, provide a crude or general set of indicators as to the state of student performance on limited variables, but it is unlikely to provide much insight into the sources of success or failure. As one Nebraska teacher told me, "You can't fatten cattle by putting them on a scale."

Why, one might ask, should such procedures seem so attractive to politicians interested in school reform? The answers are several. First, there is an appealing logic to the idea that all schools should have a common curriculum and a uniform examination system. Entertaining differences in educational values, contexts, or history when reflecting about educational aims or the content of school programs complicates matters. As consideration of context becomes increasingly salient, universal recommendations begin to fade. Attention to context, in the eyes of some, is an inefficient way to proceed.[2]

Second, there is almost a feeling of desperation among laypeople and some educators alike that the educational establishment has failed and that, as one writer put it, "We must take charge" (Finn, 1991). Taking charge means simplifying and standardizing. Without standardization, the comparative assessment of school performance is made virtually impossible, and without comparative assessment, it is very difficult to establish a ranking. Without a ranking, excellence is difficult to determine. So the idea of the race emerges: each child on the same track, jumping the same hurdles. To the victor go the spoils. Whether one track is appropriate for all children in this nation of ours or whether all children starting at the same start line when the gun goes off is a neglected consideration. Thus, our culture's not so tacit meritocracy supports the idea that in schools, as in socks, one size fits all. Ironically, this idea is often embraced in the name of educational equity, as if sameness and equity were identical.

It should not be overlooked that the aspiration to compare does not terminate with our national borders. It makes little sense talking about world-class schools if there is not a world-class race in which our children are to run, a kind of educational Olympics. To have a world-class race, one must have not only a common international assessment program; one must also have a common world curriculum. If the Japanese have a view of science education or social studies education or mathematics education that is different from our own, assessing our students on instruments appropriate for their curricula would be neither wise nor enlightening. To be interpretable (and even then with enormous difficulty) curricula as well as assessment methods must be common to the students being assessed. In the Olympics, all runners in a race compete on the same track and start at the same place. Such conditions are far from common in our own schools, let alone schools throughout the planet.[3]

There is, of course, a third reason why simple solutions appeal: they are less expensive than complicated ones. If the significant improvement of schooling were possible by measuring student achievement and making public its results, or by prescribing a common curriculum for all, then it would be unnecessary to support research into teaching and curriculum or the development of programs that try out experimental forms of school organization. If the key to success is a year-round school, or the privatization of education, or the provision of dollar incentives for achievement—the equivalent of educational piecework—the need to invest in costly R&D would evaporate. Many people believe the solutions to be simple. It was not so long ago that "back to the basics" was considered the most promising solution to our educational problems. It was a solution built upon the belief that "if it was good enough for me, it's good enough for my kids."

Regardless of the reasons or the motives driving school reform, the consequence of the inadequate analysis of the structure of schooling and the limited approach to its improvement is the seemingly ineluctable growth of teacher cynicism. For experienced teachers, the reform movement, replete with its new panaceas, is reminiscent of older, failed attempts to do something to really enhance teaching and to improve the conditions of schooling. To many teachers, the aims of the reform, couched as they are in terms of the availability of personnel and economic models of social progress, are alien to their own deep-seated motives for teaching. Having their students become number one in an educational-economic race was not what brought them into teaching in the first place and is not, for most, a persuasive rationale for their efforts in the classroom. The educational targets of the new reform (and those of the recent past) do not capture their imagination or inspire them to new ideals. Given the history of failed attempts to find a golden lever of school improvement, teachers can be excused if they are less than enthusiastic. They realize that after all the drums and cymbals have ceased, they will remain in the classroom with their students, doing the best they can under increasingly adverse conditions.

As for school administrators, they too know that reform efforts have come and gone. But school administrators are more public-vulnerable than teachers. The principal, in both an administrative and an *educational* sense, is responsible for the school; the superintendent, for the district. Neither can afford to ignore the calls for reform, and both often adopt the language of reform—"restructuring," "cooperative learning," "cognitive mapping," "integrated curriculum," "performance assessment"—without either a careful conceptual analysis of the meaning of these notions or the creation of their empirical counterparts in the school. In short, both teachers and administrators adapt, but in different ways, to the current educational passions. Such adaptation is a way to cope with a demanding public and to appear up to date.

Obstacles to Change

The thrust of my comments thus far has been to underscore the relatively feckless character of reform efforts and to relate their overall impotence to a shallow analysis of schooling and an uninspired conception of its mission. But, clearly, it must be recognized that even with the deepest analysis, it would be difficult to change schools significantly. Schools are robust institutions. Recognizing the sources of their stability is important if more adequate approaches to their improvement are to be created. It will be useful to identify some of the major foundation stones that make schools tough to change. For purposes of convenience and economy, I limit my attention to the following.

First, the images of teaching, of classrooms, and of what schools are like are learned early in life. Teaching is the only profession I can think of in which professional socialization begins at age five. As a result, those who teach have had years to internalize a set of expectations regarding what teachers do and what schools are like. To bring about significant change in schools requires, among other things, changing the images that teachers hold of their work. These new images are sometimes explored in teacher-education programs, but the fact of the matter is that most schools, from young teachers' perspectives, resemble to a very high degree the schools they attended as elementary and secondary school students. As a result, the schools in which they teach often make it difficult for their new images of teaching to take root. A program in teacher education that advocates a collaborative approach to teaching or an integrated conception of curriculum, but that places prospective teachers in schools in which that sort of teaching is virtually impossible or in which curricular integration is extremely difficult, is unlikely to achieve the aims it seeks. Furthermore, young teachers are often counseled by veteran teachers to forget what they were taught in teacher-education programs: educational reality resides in the school as it is.

Happily, the current push toward more collaborative relationships between public school teachers and university professors may ameliorate some of the difficulties new teachers encounter. As true parity develops between professors and public school teachers, a more congruent relationship between teacher education programs and the educational possibilities of schooling is likely to develop. If this, in fact, occurs, there will be, I believe, increased opportunity for significant change.[4]

Second, given the current structure of schools, teachers develop, appropriate, and invent forms of professional adaptation that enable them to cope with the numerous demands that constitute their professional life. These forms of adaptation make it possible for them to process substantial amounts of information efficiently and to organize their school day so that they are able to survive. The appropriation, development, and invention of particular pedagogical techniques, modes of classroom organization, procedures for providing information to students, ways of scoring exams, and methods for distributing opportunities to students within classrooms are all skills that teachers need to acquire in order to cope. These skills, once internalized, make it possible for teachers to focus on the substantive aspects of their own pedagogy. Yet many of these very same skills that make pedagogical survival possible are the skills that would be altered in a genuine reform effort. Thus the bind. Without well-entrenched repertoires, teaching cannot go forward. And with well-entrenched repertoires, the appropriation or invention of new skills becomes difficult. It is difficult to give up old habits when they have worked "so well" for so long. This is especially so when risk of failure for the experimental exploration of new pedagogical possibilities is likely to be professionally costly.

A third factor that stabilizes a school relates to its organizational structure. By organizational structure I mean the way in which time, space, roles, and subject matters are defined. Schools are organized structures. Their features are so common that we seem to regard them as natural, rather than as cultural artifacts that could be other than the way they are. For example, although there are some exceptions, most teachers teach about thirty students at a time; most teachers begin their work at about 8:30 A.M. and finish at about 3:00 P.M.; most schools begin the school year in September and end in June; most teachers work solo in a classroom; most subjects are taught as discrete fields of study with relatively little integration at the middle and senior high school levels; in most schools there are usually only two professional roles, teacher or school administrator; most students are given letter grades to symbolize their performance; and so on. One could travel from Maine to California, Florida to North Dakota, and most schools would display the features I have just described. The exceptions are indeed exceptions.

The structural features of schools are further reinforced with a variety of common norms. Dreeben (1968), for example, comments on the norm of universality. A child at home can be accommodated by parents in relation to individual conditions and specific contexts. In school, teachers feel the need "not to play favorites," to treat all students alike with respect to rule enforcement; the student's individual situation is submerged to norms that apply to all, and teachers are hesitant to violate those norms or to appear unfair. Dreeben also points out that grouping students by age fosters comparisons among "like kinds." Such grouping is neither a part of family life, where children of different ages coexist, or life in the neighborhood, where children of different ages play together. One could add to this list, but the point, I think, is clear. The way in which we have structured schools has substantial implications for the way people behave within them, a lesson that Roger Barker (1968) makes plain in his ecological psychology. When the structure of schooling conflicts with our aspirations or with the innovations we hope to introduce, it is likely that the structure will alter the innovation or modify the aspiration rather than the reverse. The school changes the incoming message more than the incoming message changes the school.

The school's resistance to reform is seldom adequately addressed in efforts at school reform. The search is usually for some innovation that works in the existing school structure. All the curriculum development efforts of the curriculum reform movement of the 1960s were designed to fit into the existing school structure. None of these reforms survived.

There is good reason for the robust quality of school structure. First, schools are institutions that have a strong tradition, and traditions breed expectations. We expect schools to be organized the way they are—whether or not their organization is conducive to the aims to which we aspire. Second, teachers and administrators have developed professional skills that fit the existing structure of schools. For example, the skills of teaching are virtually predicated on the assumption that the teacher will work alone in a classroom with about thirty students. Indeed, the vast amount of research on teaching is built upon such an expectation. One can only wonder about the utility or relevance of such research if the conditions within which teachers teach were to be radically changed.

Third, expectations for schools also infuse the psyches of their clients: students and parents. Those parents who have done well in traditional schools, and who "know" that the schools their children will encounter in the future will be largely like those they have known in the past, are particularly likely to be resistant to radical change. When you have been a winner or when you know the rules of the game, there is little appetite for changing the rules.

A fourth factor that stabilizes schools is the tendency to want to change them from the top down. From a bureaucratic perspective, the implementation of educational policy is a responsibility of the professional educator. Teachers and school administrators are often regarded as public servants whose job is to execute what policymakers mandate.

In a sense, this view is reasonable. Boards of education at the state and local levels *are* responsible for educational policy. It *is* their job to formulate directions and to provide guidelines. But school administrators and teachers are not simply technical personnel. They must have a hand in the shaping of policy as well as in its implementation. If teachers feel no commitment to new mandates, passive resistance is likely. With passive resistance, the probability of productive change is very small indeed. But even more, policymakers deal with elementary or secondary children in general. For policymakers, these children are abstractions. Teachers face the real thing. Unlike units rolling off an assembly line, where standardized methods can yield utterly predictable results, teachers must make intellectual adaptations not only in methods but in ends as well. Furthermore, the construction of meaning is not something that teachers do and pass on to students, but something that students do for themselves. The shape these meanings take is idiosyncratic. The personal construction of meaning, moreover, is not an educational liability (except in a system obsessed with standardized outcomes) but one of education's most prized virtues and absolutely essential for cultural viability. It is through such constructions that the commonweal is enhanced. It is through our differences that we enrich each other. The top-down bureaucratic approach to school reform typically underestimates the kind of professional latitude teachers must have to exploit their talents and to exercise the professional judgment they must employ to deal with those bundles of "individual differences" we normally refer to as "children."

The basic point here is that schooling and teaching cannot be treated as if they could be remote-controlled from afar. Teachers and school administrators who do not understand or have no commitment to change are unlikely to change. Sadly, educational reformers have neglected heeding this vital consideration.

Looking Beneath the Surface

The reform of education not only requires deeper and more comprehensive analysis of schools; it must also attend to the dimensions of schooling that must be collectively addressed to make educational reform educationally real. This attention must go well beyond changes in individual aspects of educational practice. The "latest" educational solution to educational problems needs to be regarded as one small part of a larger complex. New approaches to teaching—the development of higher order thinking skills, for example—are not likely to be realized unless curriculum and evaluation methods support educational practices aimed at such a goal. Teachers cannot devote the necessary time to engage students in inductive methods of learning if the coverage of the curriculum or achievement of high scores on tests assessing low order thinking remains, for all practical purposes, paramount. Teaching itself is unlikely to be refined as long as teachers remain in a school structure that insulates them from their colleagues or is governed by norms that are inhospitable to constructive but critical feedback. I suppose the principle I am trying to articulate here is an aesthetic principle: works of art require attention to wholes; configuration is central; everything matters. Applied to schools, it means that the school as a whole must be addressed. What we are dealing with is the creation of a culture.

In many ways the word *culture* is especially apt. A culture in the biological sense is a set of living organisms that can grow only if the medium in which they reside is hospitable to their growth. The school is that medium. The culture is the students and the adults who work with them. The growth we seek is the enlargement of mind. To create the medium they need, we need to pay attention to matters of mix. What goes into that mix surely includes the intentions that give direction to the enterprise, the structure that supports it, the curriculum that provides its content, the teaching with which that content is mediated, and the evaluation system that enables us to monitor and improve its operation. No educational reform that has been proposed has collectively addressed these primary dimensions of schooling.

To approach the reform of schools ecologically or, as others put it, systemically, requires, at the very least, attention to intentions—what aims really matter in the educational enterprise as a whole? It also requires attention to the structure of the school. The features of the workplace, as I have already argued, are of substantial importance to both teachers and students. Systemic reform requires attention to the curriculum. What is to be made available to students, and what is the basis of the selection? It requires attention to teaching. No curriculum can survive incompetent teaching, and no curriculum is worth teaching well that is not worth teaching at all. Finally, the evaluation methods employed must be addressed. To embark on the reform of schools in order to achieve particular ideals while using forms of assessment or evaluation that conflict in spirit or in fact with those ideals is to scuttle one's chances for success. Approaches to evaluation should, I believe, be grounded in a view that regards their primary function as educational (Eisner, 1985). That is, evaluation activities ought to be conceived of as educational resources designed to enhance the conditions that serve the educational purposes of the enterprise. These five dimensions—the intentional, the structural, the curricular, the pedagogical, and the evaluative—are key elements in any comprehensive, ecological, or systemic approach to school reform. To be sure, they do not exhaust the array of conditions that could be addressed—family support for schools, for example—but nevertheless they are at the core of successful reform.[5]

The preceding pages were intended to give the reader a sense of the reform efforts that have dotted our educational history since the 1960s. These efforts have not been rousing successes. Unfortunately, current efforts at reform seem no more promising. My concerns are not unique. Writing in *The Predictable Failure of Educational Reform*, Seymour Sarason (1990) says:

It is noteworthy, indeed symptomatic, that the proponents of educational reform do not talk about changing the educational system.
They will couch their reforms in terms of improving schools or the
quality of education. And if there is any doubt that they have other
than the most superficial conception of the educational system,
that doubt disappears when one examines their remedies, which
add up to "we will do what we have been doing, or what we ought
to be doing, only we will now do it better." (p. 13)

I concur with Sarason's sentiments. These concerns of ours
should not be regarded as pessimistic. What *is* pessimistic is an un-
willingness or inability to recognize the magnitude of the task, to be
sucked up into a heady but naive optimism about "what works"
(U.S. Department of Education, 1987), to hop aboard any passing
bandwagon that rolls along to the loudest music. There is no virtue
to being au courant with the educational reform movement if the
efforts are likely to be feckless or merely political accommodations
that put one comfortably in the mainstream. Sometimes more progress is made swimming upstream.

This leads me to the major focus of this book. I will not address
all of the critical considerations I have just identified. My aim is to
provide a reasoned and principled basis for deciding what to teach. It
is also to explore the implications of these ideas for teaching and
for the conduct of educational evaluation. My aim is to provide a
framework that I believe can be useful for creating truly educative
schools.

Human Nature and the Purposes of Schooling

The task of deciding what to teach is ultimately related to a vision of
human nature and an image of the purposes of schooling. To formulate intentions for schools and to define the programs that will be
made available to the young are not only key educational tasks; they
are tasks that are contentiously debated in our culture. Unlike the
situation in many other nations, where educational policies are defined at a ministerial level for the nation as a whole, the directions
that schools take in America are the result of policies belonging, by
law, to the state and, in turn, to local school boards. While there is
far greater nationalization of education in America than Americans
like to believe—especially at present—there are, as well, considerable
debate about and clearly different visions of what is possible and

desirable for schools. Any conception that I articulate in this book must compete with other visions of what schools should provide. Elsewhere, I have identified several major orientations to curriculum or, in other terms, educational ideologies (Eisner, 1985, 1991a). These orientations and ideologies provide a basis for making curriculum choices and for rationalizing educational aims. Today, the aims of schools and the content implied by these aims are rooted in the marketplace. Schools in America, we are told, must provide the work force that will make America once again competitive, and this means teaching students how to think. The idea is that in previous times students did not really need to know how to think: apparently it was not considered important, since jobs made simple demands upon workers. Schools needed to train children to endure boredom in order to inoculate them to the boredom they would surely encounter on the assembly line. Today, it seems, the new cognitive demands of the workplace and the requirements of the work force serve as the primary data sources for the formulation of educational intentions and the development of school programs. In America today, the business community is taking the lead in defining the educational agenda for American children (Berman, Weiler Associates, 1988).

By way of contrast, consider the position of those whose view of what is really important places at its center an array of theological values. Catholic schools, Orthodox Jewish schools, and fundamentalist Protestant schools are all predicated on the centrality of God's word as a basis for the design of educational programs. Schools that leave out what the Bible teaches or the church espouses cannot, in principle, be educationally adequate. Here, the major data source is not our competitive position relative to Japan or Korea, but a view of what the young need in order to lead spiritually satisfying and morally correct lives. Parents who embrace such a vision send their children to parochial schools whose programs are intended to make the realization of such values possible.

There are others who claim that the proper aim of schooling is the transmission of culture, but not just any culture, only the very best that human beings have created. The Great Books Programs, the Paideia schools, and in some ways the Coalition of Essential Schools are predicated on the idea that not all curriculum content is created equal. Differences in the quality of what humans have created are important, and one of the important tasks of the professional educator is to understand what is truly of value and to forgo teaching those "important" subjects—driver training, for example—that are not the primary responsibility of the school. Put in other terms, since there are substantial differences in the quality of ideas and works that humans have created, it is the job of the educator to make sure that the very best is made available to the young. Clearly, developmental considerations must be taken into account, but once having done so, the selection must be made with an eye to quality. This selection then becomes a kind of cultural canon, a means not only for transmitting culture but also for providing the glue that any society must have in order to hold together. In the absence of a conception of what is worth teaching and a view of the school's unique mission, the school has no basis for exclusion—it tries to do anything it is asked to do and hence loses its direction.

The foregoing conception of the mission of schooling is regarded by some as essentially conservative in nature. Using the schools to transmit the ideas and values of the past is, in effect, to sustain the culture as it is, and as it is, it is inequitable. Schools, the newer breed of school reformers argue (Giroux, 1989), should sensitize the young to the rampant social inequities that pervade society. Schools should help them become aware of the interests that lead to the destruction of the environment; they should help them understand the causes of poverty, drug abuse, unemployment, the excessive uses of energy. Put in other terms, the proper content of school curricula is located in the world in which children will live, not in the remote and passive past. The aims of schools are to enable children to do something about creating a better, more humane, more equitable society. Unless schools succeed at such a task, the gap between the haves and have-nots will increase, the level of pollution will grow, and the ability of the polity to control its own destiny will diminish. Power in the society will remain with a relatively small elite who, through privilege of social class and economic advantage, live off the labor of the working poor.

It is important to note that there are some parents who do not want the schools to address matters of value. The values that are promulgated to the young, they believe, are the province of the home, not the school. The task of the school, in a sense, is technical. It is to develop literacy and work skills; it is to introduce children to appropriate secular content; it is *not* to engage them in "values clarification." They believe that somehow schools can be value-neutral.

It does not require much insight to recognize that the process of education and the institution of schooling that is designed to facilitate that process are not value-neutral enterprises. Schools are normative institutions. They are not merely concerned with fostering human learning. They are concerned with fostering *some* kinds of human learning. The kind of learning they intend to foster is what the culture or subculture values. Some forms of learning—learning to become a racist, learning to feel incompetent, learning to hate math—are hardly educational outcomes. They might be the outcomes of schooling, but only when schools are miseducational (Dewey, 1938). A value-neutral education is an oxymoron.

As I have already suggested, the issues that are raised, in the debate about what values should guide schools—what aims are really central, what is marginal, and what has no proper place within the school's purview—are of fundamental importance. The orientations or ideologies I have identified are some of those that have guided school policy or have motivated those with an interest in education to either find or create schools that reflect their values.

It should be said that these orientations or ideologies are seldom directly infused into school programs or installed as one might install a refrigerator in a kitchen. Ideals, ideas, and ideologies typically compete for attention; they are a part of the political process. Their values are most often reflected in the metaphors we use to describe the aims or processes that we idealize. They seldom are mainstreamed into the circulatory system; they are more like the air we breathe.

This "soft infusion" should not be underestimated in importance. Often the way we use language for talking about schools is more seductive than we realize. And when the ideals guiding education are carried by metaphors used by those speaking from the highest offices in our land, the importance of authority makes them even more difficult to appraise critically. Like the fog that comes in, as Carl Sandburg once said, "on little cat's feet," before we know it we are enveloped in a fog we did not see coming.

What I often find disheartening is that scholars in education and professional educators in schools too often accept the premises of reform efforts without examining them critically. For example, the idea that schools should be assessed is gradually transformed into the idea that the nation's educational system will be improved by employing a common assessment system that will make state-by-state comparisons of student progress possible. Mississippi spends about one-half the dollars that Connecticut spends per child on education. Is it fair—putting aside more complex and deep-seated issues for the moment—to compare the performance of students in Mississippi with those of Connecticut? Is it fair to use the same yardstick and hold the same standards for children in school programs having very different levels of support? The answer seems clear, yet this is precisely what is being proposed. I will not provide further elaboration or examples. They are numerous. My point is that scholars and professionals in education have a scholarly and professional responsibility to examine critically the values embedded in the language used to motivate educational change. *America 2000* begins its text with allusions to Desert Storm. As in *A Nation at Risk,* education becomes, through analogy, a part of an international arms race and, also by analogy, our children foot soldiers in the battle. One can only wonder if a conception of education carried by metaphors grounded in conflict is likely to give us the kind of schools we want for our children.

How Shall We Decide What to Teach?

The task before us is to conceptualize a useful, indeed a compelling, basis for the construction of school programs. How shall we decide what to teach? What criteria can we appeal to? Can we get some clues from biology and from culture? Is there some way to exploit the capacities conferred upon us by our biological nature and those culturally created technologies of mind that amplify and extend our biologically given limits? And is there a way to do all this that is at once both generous and equitable? Can we use our knowledge of how human understanding is enlarged in order to build educational programs that make its varieties accessible to the young? I think there is.

One of the special features of human beings is our inherent proclivity to symbolize our experience. As far back as the Paleolithic period, around 250,000 years B.C., we find artifacts created that express the human desire to "make special" (Dissanyake, 1991) tools that had essentially practical, instrumental functions. Why the surface of a handheld cutting stone should be embellished with designs cannot be explained by the designs' contribution to improved cutting quality. People in the Paleolithic period—whom we can imagine living on the edge of survival—apparently found it important to confer a special presence to even the most functional of objects. This embellishment, this making special, represents a search for a way to make experience special by the embellishment of ordinary tools. It also displays a recognition that embellishment can evoke a special experiential state. Humans seemed to recognize that the meaning of an object could transcend its merely utilitarian features if the object received special treatment. To achieve such a status, something needed to be done to the object itself, something beyond its merely practical or instrumental function.

The rudiments of such embellishment are the beginning of the symbolic images that humans used to adorn the Lescaux caves some 40,000 years B.C. From the decorative there emerged the representational: the image could not only be employed for its own sake, it could stand for something besides itself. This recognition represents one of the most important evolutionary cultural achievements in human history. I say *cultural* because the creation of a symbol implies the presence of another, someone for whom the symbol can have meaning. Meaning shared through the creation of symbols constitutes one of the primary devices for maintaining and advancing a culture. Its rudiments appear first in those embellishments we call decoration.

The capacity to create symbols is related to the biological equipment that is an inherent part of our species. If not congenitally impaired, we possess a differentiated sensory system through which we learn to ''read'' the qualities of the environment to which the components of this system are responsive. The visual world is made conscious through the exercise of sight, the auditory world through the capacity to hear, the tactile world through the ability to feel what we touch. These biologically given capacities are the resources we use to adapt to the demands of the environment and, for humans, the resources that we employ to alter it. Our sensory system is, one might say, a kind of information pickup system. We literally get in touch with the world through our increasingly refined ability to experience the qualities of the world we inhabit.

It should not seem surprising that the content of our consciousness, mediated as it is by the ''data'' our sensory system makes available, should not also be used as a resource for the representation for experience. Sight, sound, and touch not only make it possible for us to read the scene; they also function as resources through which our experiences can be transformed into symbols. They are, I will argue, the stuff out of which *forms of representation* are created. Forms of representation are auditory, visual, kinesthetic, and gustatory; they manifest themselves in music, art, dance, speech, text, mathematics, and the like. What we choose to symbolize is rooted in our experience, and our experience, both empirical and imaginative, is influenced (but not determined) by the acuteness of our senses. The senses provide the material for the creation of consciousness, and we, in turn, use the content of consciousness and the sensory potential of

various materials to mediate, transform, and transport our consciousness into worlds beyond ourselves. In other words, forms of representation allow us to both create and enhance our private life and to
give it a public presence. By making it public, we can share that life
with others.

Looked at this way, we find a vast array of ideas portrayed in
forms that appeal to one or more sensory modalities. Music, which
to some degree is both visual and tactile, is nevertheless primarily
auditory. Poetry is used as a language to generate images and other
forms of meaning through the referents that the language implies
and the cadences poetic forms display. Film and video exploit vision,
text, and music to create meanings that no single form of representation could make possible. Over time, we have learned to expand and
refine the ways in which our consciousness can be created and to
extend the journeys it is able to take. We accomplish this feat through
the forms of representation that humans have created, forms that are
themselves made possible because of the biological capacities that we
as a species possess.

In his book *Acts of Meaning,* Jerome Bruner (1990) makes the
important point that the tools humans have invented, what he calls
"technologies of mind" or "prosthetic devices," are means for ex-
ceeding our biological limits. He writes:

> The tool kit of any culture can be described as a set of prosthetic
> devices by which human beings can exceed or even redefine the
> "natural limits" of human functioning. Human tools are precisely
> of this order—soft ones and hard ones alike. There is, for example,
> a constraining biological limit on immediate memory—George
> Miller's famous "seven plus or minus two." But we have con-
> structed symbolic devices for exceeding this limit: coding systems
> like octal digits, mnemonic devices, language tricks. Recall that
> Miller's main point in that landmark paper was that by conversion
> of input through such coding systems, we, as enculturated human
> beings, are enabled to cope with seven *chunks* of information rather
> than with seven *bits.* Our knowledge, then, becomes enculturated
> knowledge, indefinable save in a culturally based system of nota-
> tion. In the process, we have broken through the original bounds
> set by the so-called biology of memory. Biology constrains, but not
> forevermore. (p. 21)

Bruner's point is of critical importance for education. While our
biological endowment affords our species the capacities to experience
the environment, it is through culture that these capacities are ex-

tended or amplified. The forms of representation that humans have invented—writing, for example—have made it possible to create an indelible record of aspects of our experience, a record that memory alone could not sustain. Maps allow us to see a world we cannot see. These forms both stabilize our experience by fixing it in some medium and transport us psychologically to places we can encounter only through the forms of representation that populate our culture. Through music, painting, poetry, and story, we can participate in worlds that would otherwise be closed to us. The meanings secured through poetry, painting, music, and story, through the sciences and mathematics, have their own special content. They perform unique epistemic functions *if* we are able to "read" their content.

The lesson here for education is, to my way of thinking, both clear and consequential. Since meaning in the context of representation is always mediated through some form of representation, each form of representation has a special contribution to make to human experience. We see this daily in our own culture: we use different forms to say different things. Education, I believe, ought to enable the young to learn how to access the meanings that have been created through what I have referred to as forms of representation. But access to the meanings others have created is not enough. Education ought to help the young learn how to create their own meanings through these forms. Schools cannot accomplish these aims unless the curriculum they provide offers students opportunities to become, for want of a better term, multiliterate. Without the ability to "read" the special and unique meanings that different forms of representation make possible, their content will remain for them an untappable resource, an enigma that they cannot solve. The remainder of the book is devoted to the case for using this view of meaning and mind for building school programs. It is a case rooted in our biological nature and in the achievements of our culture. For this case to be made, we must start with the first avenue to our consciousness—our senses. Chapter 2 explores their contributions to our conceptual life.

2 The Role of the Senses in Concept Formation

The aims of schooling and the development of the student's ability to think and to know have long been associated. Indeed, if there is any general educational goal to which both professional educators and the lay public subscribe, it is in what the literature refers to as "cognitive development" (Downey, 1960). The focus on the development of cognition as an educational goal is, I believe, quite appropriate; schools as institutions and education as a process ought to foster the student's ability to understand the world, to deal effectively with problems, and to acquire wide varieties of meaning from interactions with it. The development of cognition is the primary means to these ends. But just what is cognition, and what is not? What constitutes cognitive activity, and what kinds of activities are noncognitive? Unfortunately, cognition is often narrowly conceived.[1] Perhaps nowhere does this problem stand out more clearly than when cognition is contrasted with affect. Affect is supposed to deal with feeling and not with knowing, while cognition supposedly deals with knowing and not with feeling.

If such distinctions were simply theoretical conveniences, they might not cause as much practical mischief. The mischief stems from the fact that the distinctions are reified and practically applied. The cognitive and the affective are all too often regarded as distinct and independent states of the human organism. Such distinctions manifest themselves educationally in decisions that are made about the content of the curriculum and when aspects of that content shall be taught. It is maintained, for example, that cognitive studies, those studies that require students to think, should be taught when they are fresh and alert since thinking, as contrasted with feeling, is demanding. Hence, subjects regarded as cognitive are taught in the morning, while those that are believed to be affective—the fine arts, for example—are taught (if at all) in the afternoon, often at the end of the week. What happens is that the limited view of cognition that permeates so much psychological and educational literature legitimates a form of educational practice that itself limits what children have the opportunity to learn in school. Consider its impact on the use of time in school.

Time-on-task research indicates that time is differentially allocated to different areas of study. The absolute amount of time devoted to particular subjects is not, however, the only factor that influences what children learn. *When* subjects are taught is also important. Thus, because some subjects are not only given the lion's share of attention but also given "prime time," decisions that are made about the use of time in the curriculum not only affect the student's access to particular content, they also convey to students what is regarded as important and what is not. If it were true that some subjects were noncognitive and if one believed that schools should emphasize the development of cognitive ability, one could make a case for allocating prime time to content areas that were cognitive. This case cannot be made because the hard and fast distinction between what is cognitive and what is affective is itself faulty. There can be no affective activity without cognition. If to cognize is to know, then to have a feeling and not to know it is not to have it. At the very least, in order to have a feeling one must be able to distinguish between one state of being and another. The making of this distinction is the product of thinking, a product that itself represents a state of knowing.

Similarly, there can be no cognitive activity that is not also affective.[2] Even if it were possible to think in a way that was void of feeling, such a state could be known only by knowing the feeling that the absence of feeling signifies. Although this appears to be paradoxical, it is not. To experience thought as bland, dull, boring, feckless—in short, as feeling less—is to recognize its feelingful character. When one's cognitive processes are permeated by other feeling tones, other affective qualities are obviously at work. In short, affect and cognition are not independent processes; nor are they processes that can be separated. They interpenetrate just as mass and weight do. They are part of the same reality in human experience.

Toward a Wider View of Cognition

My purpose in emphasizing the interdependence of cognition and affect is to illuminate the theoretical tradition that pervades our beliefs about human thought and to illustrate a few of the ways in which that tradition affects school curricula. A view of cognition that restricts thinking and knowing to forms of mentation that are exclusively discursive or mathematical leaves out far more than it includes. When such a conception then becomes extended so that human intelligence itself is defined by operations employing only, or even mainly, those forms of thinking, the liabilities of the view for education are multiplied even further. On this matter, John Dewey had some important things to say. Speaking of the relationship of intelligence to art, a so-called affective area, Dewey (1934/1958) wrote:

> Any idea that ignores the necessary role of intelligence in production of works of art is based upon identification of thinking with use of one special kind of material, verbal signs and words. To think effectively in terms of relations of qualities is as severe a demand upon thought as to think in terms of symbols, verbal and mathematical. Indeed, since words are easily manipulated in mechanical ways, the production of a work of genuine art probably demands more intelligence than does most of the so-called thinking that goes on among those who pride themselves on being ''intellectuals.'' (p. 46)

Dewey's views were originally published in 1934 in a book that he wrote when he was more than seventy years old. *Art as Experience* is one of the last major works of his career, and yet it is largely unread in educational and psychological circles. The wide view of cognition that it portrays somehow never took root in mainstream educational or psychological theory.

What would a wider view of cognition look like? What would it suggest for the curriculum of the school and for educational evaluation? What new forms of intelligence might be recognized through it? What abilities would surface as children now regarded as nonintellectual became appreciated? How might such a view alter the kinds of questions that are now raised and studied concerning human abilities?

Many of the issues that I have identified are closely related to Gardner's (1983) work on multiple intelligences. Gardner is also concerned with the ways in which individuals address different kinds of problems and with their differential aptitude for solving problems of different kinds. He is interested in the developmental features of each of seven types of intelligence and in the characteristics of the cultures that encourage the development of each. However, Gardner's work and mine have an important difference. I am concerned with matters of meaning and with the different kinds of meaning that different forms of representation make possible. This book addresses itself to the ways in which different kinds of meaning can be secured and the conditions within curriculum and teaching that foster what might be regarded as multiple forms of literacy. What does it mean to secure poetic meaning, and what does poetic meaning help one understand? What kinds of meanings are accessible through the visual world? And how does one learn to read those meanings, not only within what we call works of art but within the environment at large? The curriculum that is made available to students in school is, in an essential sense, a means through which students can learn to encode and decode the meanings made possible through different forms of representation. Through this process, different kinds of intelligences are cultivated or, more broadly, cognition itself is expanded.

It should be remembered that the tendency to regard cognition as something independent of both "sense data" and feeling has a long history.[3] Plato (1951) regarded knowledge that was dependent on the senses as untrustworthy and believed affect to be a seductive distraction that kept one from knowing the truth. Only pure thought unencumbered by feeling and by sense data could make it possible to know what was true. *Episteme*—the Greek term for knowledge— was the result of a rational, not an empirical, process. Mathematics and dialectics were its foremost vehicles since both depended upon the use of "pure" reason (see Popper, 1945). The tendency to separate the cognitive from the affective is reflected in our separation of the mind from the body, of thinking from feeling, and the way we have dichotomized the work of the head from the work of the hand. What might seem at first to be abstract distinctions that have little bearing upon the real world in which we live turn out to shape not only our conception of mind but our educational policies as well. Students who are good with their hands might be regarded as talented, but seldom as intelligent. Those who are emotive, sensitive, or imaginative might have aptitudes for the arts, but the "really bright" go into mathematics or the sciences. In some states those who are considered "intelligent," as defined by their IQ, receive state funds to enhance their educational development. Those who are merely "talented" do not. Such distinctions in policy and in theory do not, in my view, do justice either to the children or to the society. More suitable curriculum policy might be formulated by appealing to a wider conception of mind and by formulating educational programs that are designed to expand its power. The place one might begin to develop a wider conception of mind is by examining the function of the senses and identifying the role they play in the achievement of mind.

The Sources of Experience

All biological organisms possess means through which they establish contact with the environment. Even a single-cell amoeba is able to respond to and incorporate the life-sustaining resources that come into its midst. The human organism has, of course, an extraordinarily more varied sensory apparatus for making contact with the world. Each sensory system is constructed to pick up information about some, but not all, of the qualities that constitute the immediate environment (Neisser, 1976). Thus, the organism's visual sensory system is designed to be sensitive to light. Given a normally functioning visual system, the organism has the capacity to discriminate among the qualities that constitute the visual world and to use the data secured to make inferences about it. The capacity of the human organism to differentiate among the qualities of the environment, to recall them in memory, and to manipulate them in the imagination is biologically rooted. As long as the particular sensory systems the human possesses are intact, the individual can learn how to differentiate, to recall, and to manipulate the qualities he or she encounters. Furthermore, the extent to which sensory systems can be used to distinguish among those qualities to which they are biologically sensitive depends part on the organism's prior experience and developmental history. For example, the four-week-old infant must learn how to focus and how to track moving objects, but so must the forty-year-old adult who is first learning how to hunt. While the adult has all of the physiological prerequisites, other necessary conditions—prior hunting experience, for example—may be missing. As for the infant, *both* the physiological and the experiential conditions that are lacking will soon be gained, for, at about the age of four months, both the ability to focus and to track are well-developed skills in the normal child (White, 1971).

But imagine for a moment the situation if a child were congenitally blind or for some reason unable to secure tactile sensation. Suppose that child had never experienced light and that even its tongue was insensitive to tactile quality. What could the child know about the visual or the tactile? What could it remember of those qualities? To what extent could it create through its imagination what it had never had an opportunity to experience? There is no reason to believe that anything in these dimensions of experience could be secured. Consider an analogy.

Suppose we assume for a moment that each of us reading these pages was required from birth to wear red filters over our eyes. What, under such conditions, could we come to know of the colors of the environment? What would we make of our experience? What would we know about what we were unable to see? It would be difficult even to make inferences about this loss since we would not know what we had missed. Without access to what fully functioning sight provides, we would be unable even to speculate upon the character or magnitude of our loss.

Most of us assume, of course, that, by and large, we can experience most of what the world has to offer. Most of us have our senses intact, and in varying degrees we have learned to use them. Indeed, our conception of the world does not exceed what our senses have made possible. Even the smallest subparticle of the atom and the black holes of space, phenomena that no one has ever seen, are imaginable, visually illustrated or illustratable. Through imagination—the creation of mental images—we are able to conceive what we have never experienced in the empirical world. These images are themselves created out of the empirical qualities to which our senses are responsive.

The contributions of vision to conception and imagination are not contributions limited to vision alone. Each sensory system makes its own unique contributions. Indeed, because each system functions specifically in relation to certain qualities, there is no way in which one sensory system can completely compensate for the absence of another. Even synesthesia depends upon the recall of the particular qualities that individual sensory systems make possible.

Although one's ability to use the sensory systems as avenues for experience is affected by maturation, the manner in which such abilities are used is affected by far more than maturation. What one is able to experience through any of the sensory systems depends, for example, not only on the characteristics of the qualities in the environment but also on one's purposes, frames of reference, or what Neisser (1976) refers to as the anticipatory schemata that the individual has acquired during the course of his or her life. Perception, as

Neisser puts it, is a cognitive event. Just how factors such as prior learning and expectation affect one's perception of the world will be discussed later. The main point here is that the sentient human is not simply a passive material that, like moist clay, receives the impress of the empirical world, but is an active agent that selects and organizes aspects of that world for cognition (see Dewey, 1938; Piaget, 1977).

The reciprocity between what the organism does to the world and what the world does to the organism is dramatically illustrated by cross-cultural research on perception and by work on sensory deprivation. With respect to the latter, it has been found that the absence of light during the course of maturation can have irreversible effects on an organism's ability to see. Kittens between four and twelve weeks of age, whose eyes have been occluded, are unable to see when the occlusions are removed (Kuffler & Nicolls, 1976). Lack of access to light during critical periods of development has a nonreversible impact on a kitten's sight. Even with the occlusions removed, the kitten remains blind. What this research suggests is that the firing of certain neurons requires an environmental trigger, the absence of which leaves them in a latent condition that, beyond a critical period, renders them inoperable. The concept of readiness here suggests that if an organism does not have opportunities to use certain capacities at critical periods in its life, it will not be able to use them once that period has passed.

This research was, of course, performed on kittens, but it is suggestive of questions having to do with the kinds of opportunities provided to children in school and in the culture at large. What kinds of stimuli do we fail to provide in schools, and what abilities do we, therefore, neglect developing? What are the long-range consequences of such neglect? If one had a map of the mind that identified the varieties of cognitive capacity that human beings possess, it might be possible to describe the qualities and tasks encountered in the environment in relation to those capacities. If one were then able to plot the incidence of their use within a culture—or a school—one would, in principle, be able to determine the magnitude of the opportunities the culture or the school provided for particular capacities to be developed. Perhaps we would find that each home and each subculture, as well as each culture, provide different opportunities for individuals to achieve particular forms of mental competence (Cole, 1974).

Although the research described places great emphasis on the contributions of environmental conditions to stimulate or provide the organism with the opportunity to use certain capacities, the way in which an organism treats the qualities that make up the environment are not simply a function of the qualities as such. *Which* particular qualities the organism chooses to attend to and *how* he or she decides to respond are not completely influenced by the qualities themselves. A bridge, for example, can be perceived as a structure to serve as the theme for a poem or as a means for calculating height or length, or for estimating the amount of time it will take to cross at forty-seven miles per hour. Research on hemispheric specialization suggests that different brain functions will be utilized in dealing with each of these tasks (Gazzaniga & Sperry, 1967). It is likely, furthermore, that what an individual knows how to do and what he or she enjoys doing creates a response tendency that increases the probability that certain modes of thought will become characteristic. The painter will characteristically view the bridge as an expressive form having shape, scale, and color or as a candidate for a painting. The poet is likely to view the bridge as subject matter for a poem or epigram. The engineer regards it as an achievement in managing stress. Each construes the bridge in different terms, the terms with which each is most competent. As Ernst Gombrich once observed: ''The painter does not paint what he can see, he sees what he is able to paint.''

One can only speculate on the unintended consequences of competency on the development of human capacity. Might it be that the development of certain competencies are achieved only at the cost of allowing others to atrophy?

What we have noted thus far is not only that there is a transactional or reciprocal relationship between the qualities of the environment and the cognitive structures or anticipatory schemata a person possesses, but also that perception itself is constructive. This point has been mentioned earlier, but it is worth emphasizing particularly because the constructive character of perception has been underplayed in some psychological theories. Consider, for example, that in some psychological theories the qualities that constitute the environment are referred to as stimuli.[4] As a term, *stimuli* suggests that environmental conditions are the major, if not the sole, determinant of the response. What the concept of stimulus neglects is that what constitutes a stimulus, that is, what stimulates, is itself a function of how the qualities that make up the so-called stimulus are perceived. Like the term *input*, which almost automatically suggests the term *output*, the term *stimulus* almost automatically suggests *response*, implying very little in the way of an intervening or mediating process. Such a theoretical view implies that the major focus of experimental attention should be upon the qualities of the stimulus rather than on the frames of reference the organism is likely to use to construe its qualities. When one is conducting experiments upon organisms much simpler than humans, such a theoretical framework might have utility. With humans, it can only lead to vastly oversimplified conceptions of the sources of human action.[5]

The move away from theories of mental structure as a way of understanding human activity was initially motivated by the desire to make psychological inquiry scientifically empirical; introspection was considered unreliable, and the "mind" was too close to the metaphysics discussed in departments of philosophy. If psychology was to become scientifically respectable, neither introspection nor metaphysics would do.[6] Yet what can a psychology be that neglects the mind? Happily psychologists are returning to the study of mental life and, in the process, they are employing ingenious methods to describe and interpret how the mind functions.

Among those engaged in such work is Roger Shepard (1982), who has made the dominant focus of his research the study of mental images. Others include Pylyshyn (1986), Salomon (1979), and, from a broader social perspective, Bruner (1990). All indications suggest that mind has returned to American psychology and that the social conditions that influence its functions are increasingly becoming the object of research in the social sciences. In light of the strong behaviorist orientation that characterized the dominant mood of American psychology from John Watson to B. F. Skinner, this resurgence of interest in the mental is a promising development for those of us interested in the capacities of the educational process to foster the growth of mind.

Thus far, I have tried to identify some of the contributions the senses make to our awareness of the environment. I have also tried to identify the links between what is regarded as sense data and cognition. Because the senses have often been separated from the mind, their contributions to thinking have often been unappreciated. Activities that appear to rely upon the use of the senses or upon affect are often regarded as nonintellectual, that is, as activities that make little demand upon thinking or human intelligence. This tradition, one that is reflected not only in our psychological discourse but in our educational policies, is based upon a limited and, I believe, educationally counterproductive view of mind. The formation of concepts depends upon the construction of images derived from the material the senses provide. Such concepts are developed from the qualities possessed by particulars from which general schemata are construed.

Language and Concept Formation

Why is it that knowing is related in a fundamental way to the experience that the senses make possible? Simply because experience always requires a content. One must be able to experience something in order to know it. Even the experience of nothingness depends upon our ability to imagine the qualities of a void. Because experience is a necessary condition for knowing, and because the character of experience is dependent upon the qualities to which it is directed, the quality of experience will depend upon what our senses have access to and upon how well we are able to use them.

Such a view of knowing and concept formation seems to leave little room for the function of language, something that some hold to be the sine qua non of both thinking and knowing. I want to argue that propositional language functions largely as a surrogate for experience with qualitative material (Arnheim, 1969). We have a vocabulary that we use to refer to the qualities of the world, but this vocabulary is only a general representation of the qualities themselves. In fact, we are able to differentiate thousands of qualities for which we have no vocabulary. The same is true for grammatical construction—sentences or phrases. We operate by using language as it is conventionally defined, and in doing so we get along quite well. But even here what phrases mean is dependent upon our ability to recall the referents of the terms and the relations that hold among them. Indeed, metaphors like "I'll pick you up tomorrow" are understood not because a person will actually be picked up but because picking up objects and giving a person a "lift" have much in common. In both cases the common attributes of the referents as sources of experience (being "picked up" and giving someone "a lift") allow us to invent metaphors that relate quite comfortably to them.

Following Sir Herbert Read (1945), I am arguing that the refinement of the senses is a primary means for expanding our consciousness.[7] Learning how to represent what we have experienced is a primary means for contributing to the expanded consciousness of others. Thus, a culture or a school program that dulls the senses by neglect or disrespect thwarts the development of human aptitude and undermines the possibilities of the human mind.

This point is worth special emphasis because of the tradition that argues that concept formation is always dependent upon the use of discursive language. According to some, there can be no thinking without the use of discourse because it is not possible to form a concept that is not itself linguistic. Adam Schaff (1973) makes this point this way:

> When we adopt the monistic standpoint, we reject the claim that language and thinking can exist separately and independently of one another. Of course, we are talking about specifically *human* thinking, in other words about *conceptual* thinking. Thus we assert that in the process of cognition and communication, thinking and using a language are inseparable elements of one and the same whole. Integration is so perfect and interdependence is so precise that neither element can ever occur independently, in a "pure" form. That is precisely why the functions of thinking and language may not be treated separately, let alone contrasted with one another. (p. 118)

Such a view of thinking appears to me to be questionable on several counts. What, for example, does one do to explain the work of artists, composers, athletes, cooks, and others whose primary form of representation depends on the creation of qualitative relationships? Is it really the case, for example, that Bach had to conceptualize the Brandenberg Concertos in words before he was able to transform the words into music? Perhaps Bach's musical achievements were not a product of thinking at all? But, if this is the case, what were they due to? Inspiration? The muse, perhaps? Such explanations will hardly do. Even Noam Chomsky (1973), for whom discursive language plays a central role in the operation of mind, recognizes that thinking exceeds the limits of discourse. He writes:

> Is it the case, for example, that humans necessarily think in language? Obvious counterexamples immediately come to mind. Our only evidence of any substance is introspective, the introspection surely tells me that when I think about a trip to Paris or a camping expedition to the Rockies, the few scraps of internal monologue that may be detected hardly convey, or even suggest the content of my thought. In struggling with a mathematical problem, one is often aware of the role of a physical, geometrical intuition that is hardly expressible in words, even with effort and attention. (p. v)

The point that Chomsky is making about the fact that language does not exhaust the activities we refer to as thinking is significant for several reasons. First, it challenges the widely held belief that thinking *requires* discursive or mathematical mediation. What Chomsky recognizes is that the forms of human thought are multiple and that language in its conventional sense is only one among many of the forms that it employs. Second, it suggests that thinking and experiencing cannot be easily separated. I believe that no form of experience is possible without cognitive activity and that such activity is itself what we mean by thinking. Even the awareness of sensation requires some modicum of thought, for what else would make awareness possible? Once we recognize that perception is a cognitive event, the hard and fast distinctions among sensation, perception, and cognition begin to blur (Neisser, 1976). The behaviors that do not require one to think are those that are a function of the reflex response: the knee jerk, the eye wink, the dilation of the pupil in the eye. But *experiencing* the qualities of sound, of touch, of taste requires attention, selection, comparison, and judgment. It is very easy for someone to miss experiencing the qualities in his or her perceptual field. When we say that some people do not learn from their experience, it is because we ourselves fail to recognize that the experience we assume they are having, from which they might learn, they, in fact, are missing. Not to see the connection between an act and its consequences—something that frequently happens when one is trying to learn—is not to have a particular kind of experience, the experience represented by the recognition of the relationship.

An Expanded View of Knowledge

The reader will note that I am arguing that knowing depends upon experience, either the kind of experience that emanates from the sentient being's contact with the qualities of the environment or from the experiences born of the imagination. My use of the term *knowing* differs from the concept of knowledge as used by philosophers of either an analytic or a positivistic orientation. In more conventional usage, the term *knowledge* is restricted to a "warranted assertion" (Ayer, n.d.), of which there are two kinds: analytic and synthetic. Analytic assertions are propositions that are true by definition, such as those used in symbolic logic and in mathematics; $30 \times 20 = 600$ is an example of an analytic assertion or proposition. Such propositions are regarded as true or false if they are or are not consistent with certain axioms defined within the system. Here consistency, rather than empirical verification, is the means for determining the meaning and truthfulness of the proposition. We regard $2 + 2 = 4$

as true, not by examining the contents of the world but by understanding our agreement to use terms in a particular way.

Synthetic propositions are assertions about empirical conditions that can be falsified through specific operations that a community of competent inquirers can employ. What counts as knowledge are propositions about the world that are capable of falsification but that have not been falsified. Notice that in this conception of knowledge the role of the proposition is crucial. There can be no knowledge unless an assertion or claim about some empirical matter has been made, and assertions always require propositional form. But even more, the assertion must be capable in principle of being falsified by a set of operationally defined methods. Thus, the claim that there are fourteen cars on the parking lot can be verified by anyone who knows what cars are like, what parking lots are like, and how to count. If methods of verification cannot be employed or *in principle* imagined, the assertion is regarded simply as an utterance, something that is literally without meaning.

The reason this view of knowledge has been so attractive to so many is because by regarding knowledge as propositional and by requiring publicly available tests of its validity, it was believed possible to rid philosophy of metaphysics and unverifiable utterance— sources of confusion and obscurantism. Both positivistic and linguistic analysis were a kind of linguistic hygiene that eliminated the dross from philosophic literature.

But note that for synthetic propositions the referents for the propositions are still nonpropositional matters; they are qualities that the sensory systems pick up. Cars and parking lots are sensory before they are linguistic. In this sense, talk about those qualities is not the same as experience itself. When they are described through discourse, a reduction occurs, particularly when the talk is propositional rather than literary or poetic. In some cases, the reduction is radical. Thus, a dilemma emerges. As one moves away from propositions and operational procedures as conditions necessary for falsification, the prospects for securing consensus about the validity of claims is diminished. Yet to restrict the term *knowledge* and, by implication, *knowing* to what propositions about qualities can reveal is to exclude from the arena of knowledge all that propositions as a form of representation cannot embody. That price, in my view, is too high. Shakespeare's rendering of jealousy in *Othello*, Picasso's revelations of the horror of Guernica, Schiller's ''Ode to Joy'' cannot be reduced to propositions. The concern for validation and falsification has been so great that all else simply was regarded as suspect at best. For some, not even *that* level of cognitive status is attained since "suspect" implies that a nonlinguistic form of representation can, in principle, provide meaningful information about the world. Some would not regard anything as meaningful that cannot be refuted by "objective" operational procedures.

The educational and political ramifications of the views I have described are not simply the playthings of philosophers. They are far more than educational or philosophic exotica. Commitment to a particular view of knowledge has consequences not only for school curricula, but also for the conduct of research, for the funding of research, for promotion at universities, for the definition of professional competence, for access to publication in professional journals, and even, as I have suggested earlier, for shaping our conception of mind.[8]

In pointing out the limitations of the view of knowledge I have just described, I am not suggesting that propositions about the world have nothing to tell us or that their information load is necessarily small. I am saying, first, that propositions about empirical matters must relate to those matters through direct contact or through imagination to be meaningful and, second, that propositions as *one* form of representation cannot in principle contain all that can be known or experienced about the empirical world. Furthermore, the restriction of knowledge and, by implication, understanding to propositional discourse about the phenomenal world limits our view of reality and has a wide array of ancillary political and educational consequences that are deleterious to the development of human ability and to human understanding. I am attempting in this book to argue the case for a more general view of the forms that make diverse kinds of understanding possible in the hope that, with such a view, a wider conception of curriculum and evaluation can be forged. Methodological dogmatism, even in the name of truth, can fetter our capacity to know.

The view that knowing must be embodied within propositions leads to the belief that certain modes of thought are cognitive and intelligent, while others are affective or emotive. Meaning is the product of the one, and expressiveness is the product of the other. The sciences become the avenue to truth, and the arts the roads to pleasure and emotional release. Understanding is the exclusive issue of verified propositions, and poetic statement is regarded as noncognitive.

I find this view of knowing and of thinking curious. One's experience of the world is basically qualitative. Concepts initiate in the forms of experience that the senses make possible. When they are rendered into discourse, a transformation takes place: there is always a reduction in the process. The forms of conceptualization from one to the other are not the same. To hold that it is the discursive reduction that carries the meaning, and that the content that gives meaning to the discourse is meaningless, is to put the cart before the horse. In the desire to tame and harness meaning so that it abides by conventional rules for purposes of verification, those forms of knowing that lie outside the realm in which such rules can be applied have been made "noncognitive."

Are There Nonqualitative Concepts?

But, one might legitimately ask, are all concepts at base qualitative? What about concepts that apparently are not tied directly to the qualities of the world, concepts such as *infinity, category, nation, justice, hope.* We typically use such terms without needing to think of their referents. We communicate with an automaticity that does not take time for concrete exemplification. But this bypassing of the qualities to which the term refers should not be taken to mean that, because the term is a so-called abstraction (all terms are abstract), it is not rooted in sensory material. Suppose someone did not understand the meaning of the term *infinity* and wanted you to help him grasp its meaning. The task you would probably undertake would be to illustrate the meaning of the concept through material that was visual or visualizable. We attempt to make verbal labels meaningful by providing the label with a content that someone can experience directly or can imagine, an image that makes the construction of meaning possible. Indeed, one might well ask whether it is possible to derive any meaning whatsoever from a label if the content to which that label refers cannot be conceptualized, that is, imagined.

It is interesting to observe that the significance of the role played by the senses in conception is revealed in the Latin root of the term *intuition.* That root is *intuitus,* which means "to look upon" (*Oxford English Dictionary,* 1961). To have intuition is to have insight, to see something that was once unseen, to grasp through the senses. Hence, once having an idea explained, a person might exclaim, "I see!" signifying a grasp of the image that gives the explanation meaning.

Because concept formation occurs within and among each of the sensory systems, contacts with the environment, the way that environment is known will be largely influenced by the particular sensory system or systems we use in dealing with it. The objects that populate the environment almost always possess qualities that can be experienced by using a variety of sensory systems. A rose is not just its aroma, but also its color and texture and the relationship of these qualities to one another. A person is not simply his visual appearance, but his voice, the distinctive character of his personal traits, the sound of his walk. Even perfume is known by more than its scent; the identification of the scent with the form of the bottle in which it is packaged is of crucial importance to perfume manufacturers as well as to those who buy perfume. Even Joy, reputedly the world's most expensive perfume, would not be likely to sell well, even at bargain prices, if it were packaged in a yogurt container. The fact that the qualities of the environment are multiple means that the ways in which these qualities can be known are also potentially multiple. Refining the student's ability to experience the multiplicity of environmental qualities is one of the aims I believe educational programs should attempt to achieve.

Insofar as the qualities of the world are multiple and insofar as concept formation with respect to those qualities is multiple, it is unlikely that one's conception of complex qualitative wholes is likely to be singular. What, for example, does it mean to have a conception of autumn? For some, it is something that begins during the ninth month of the Gregorian calendar; for others, it is that period during the year when daylight diminishes and darkness expands. For teachers, I suppose, autumn means the appearance of thirty new faces and the beginning of a new school year. Autumn can also be the time in which the sharp chill of the early evening blends magically with the aroma of burning leaves. For those not tied to the restrictions of a dictionary, autumn is a multiplicity of meanings, each the offspring of how the season is experienced.

Summary and Significance

What, then, are the major points addressed thus far? First, that concept formation is itself biologically rooted in the sensory systems that humans possess. Our ability to experience different qualities constituting the environment through the information pickup systems represented by our senses provides the material out of which concepts are made. Thus, concepts are formed not only in visual, but in gustatory, olfactory, tactile, and auditory form. We have a conception of roundness not only because we know what a circle or a sphere looks like but because we know how it feels.

Second, the kinds of meanings we secure are affected by our purposes, the frames of reference we use, and the degree of differentiation we have achieved. What we experience depends in part on what nets we cast. Third, for an idea to be meaningful—say, the idea of random mutation and natural selection—the organism must initially be able to imagine or recall the referents for the terms that collectively express the idea. Randomness, for example, is the specific qualitative characteristic of a process or the characteristics of the product of that process. When distributions do not possess the characteristics one expects from a process that purports to be random, we examine the process in order to check. In the end, it is the congruence between the term and the qualities that we experience that provides warrant for the label *random*.

Similarly, a genetic mutation is recognized because it is qualitatively different from its genetic parents. Again, it is the qualities that constitute our conception of mutation that enable us to justify claims about a particular gene being a mutant. Even when an idea or concept has no empirical referent—subatomic particles, the *initial* conceptualization of DNA as a double helix, and so forth—the concept or idea is conceivable as an imaginative construction. Seen in this way, inferences and hypotheses are derived for purposes of experimentation. Even in what is regarded as the most abstract of fields, mathematics, images are at work. Einstein described his own psychological processes in this regard:

> The words or the language, as they are written or spoken, do not seem to play any role in my mechanism of thought. The psychical entities which seem to serve as elements in thought are certain signs and more or less clear images which can be "voluntarily" reproduced or combined. . . . But taken from a psychological viewpoint, this combinatory play seems to be the essential feature in productive thought—before there is any connection with logical construction in words or other kinds of signs which can be communicated to others. The above-mentioned elements are, in my case, of visual and some of muscular type. Conventional words or other signs have to be sought for laboriously only in a secondary stage, when the mentioned associative play is sufficiently established and can be produced at will. (Hadamard, 1949, p. 142)

The utilities of visualization in mathematical inquiry and scientific research appear to be straightforward. With visualization, complex relationships can be reflected upon in space rather than in time.

With qualities arrayed in space, certain relationships can be examined, the load on memory reduced, and forms of conceptual manipulation are made possible that would be very cumbersome if a linear, temporal mode of thought needed to be employed. Indeed, the utilities of such thinking are evidenced in the use of holography and through computer displays that produce images that help researchers understand relationships that could not be grasped in any other way.[9]

A fourth point is that while the kinds of concepts that are made possible through the several sensory systems can occur simultaneously, only one concept in the same sensory system can be experienced at the same time. For example, we are able to imagine a speech being given, hear the words being spoken, and see the setting in which it occurs. We are able to conceive of a melody and place the locale in which it takes place or which it expresses; program music is composed to generate such experience. But what we cannot do is to imagine two melodies simultaneously. We might shift our attention from one to the other, but we cannot experience both at once. Similarly, we cannot experience two visual images in the same conceptual space at once. We are able to imagine a complex visual array, one made up of a variety of visual elements, but we are unable to visualize red and yellow squares that occupy the same conceptual space in our imagination. The ability to employ different forms of conceptualization simultaneously has, of course, extremely important assets. Being able to visualize, to hear, and to feel, through imagination, aspects of a situation or problem with which we have to cope provides us with opportunities for rehearsal. We can play out in our imaginative life what we would otherwise have to act upon in order to know. We can stop and think in a context where the imaginative checking out of alternatives is possible before those alternatives are pursued in the empirical world. The *Gedanken*, or thought, experiment is, in the sciences, the paradigm case of such activity. Less sophisticated beginnings of such activity are to be found under more ordinary circumstances: the daydreaming of children and adults, the planning of summer holidays in winter, reflection on choices of furniture and clothing, the multitude of pensive activities that fill our waking hours. The fact that we are not restricted to one mode of conceptualization at a time allows us to secure a fuller picture of the conditions with which we must deal and makes it possible to treat them experientially as ideas before we take action.

Is the ability to engage in such thinking something schools can develop? Can we increase our skill in imaginative conceptualization through schooling? If we could, what might be the consequences of such newly developed skills? Would they contribute to the solution of problems that now appear unresolvable? To what extent, for example, does productive mathematical thinking depend upon one's ability to use skills such as visualization? Such questions are of central importance to the formation of curriculum policy. But before attempting to explore some answers, it is necessary to examine the other side of the conceptual coin, the manner in which concepts take public form and the contributions that they in turn make to cognition. For this, we turn to the process of representation.

3 Forms of Representation

Some of the ways in which the sensory system contributes to the formation of concepts were discussed in the previous chapter. But concepts, regardless of the sensory form they take, are personal aspects of human experience, and although they might provide illumination for those who have them, they are private and cannot be shared until they are made public. It is only when those experiences serve as the content for human expression that communication is possible and that the content of the experience is made social.

The Features and Functions of Forms of Representation

In order to achieve a social dimension in human experience, a means must be found to carry what is private forward into the public realm. This is achieved by employing what in this book is called *forms of representation*. Forms of representation are the devices that humans use to make public conceptions that are privately held. They are the vehicles through which concepts that are visual, auditory, kinesthetic, olfactory, gustatory, and tactile are given public status. This public status might take the form of words, pictures, music, mathematics, dance, and the like.

Consider the task of the painter. Imagine a painter taking a trip through a small midwestern town, say with a population of about 1,500. The town is located in Kansas, and the painter was born and raised in New York City. For him, the experience of the town is altogether special: the scale of the main street, the character of the

39

storefronts, the pace and comportment of the people, the menus posted on the door of the diner, the slow-paced movement of the traffic in the streets, the expanse of sky that hangs cloudless overhead. There is, for him, a special kind of magic to the place; in certain respects it is a sort of throwback to a life that he occasionally glimpsed as a boy growing up in New York, but which has long since passed.

The qualities of his experience are multiple in form and meaning. They are a mixture of images, sounds, textures, words, and the pervasive quiet brightness that seems to be everywhere. Upon reflection, he finds that his experience is punctuated at the beginning and at the end. It is bracketed in his imagination as a special event, "an object" to be recalled, an experience undergone in the spring of 1990. Intoxicated by it, he is moved to put on canvas and thus to stabilize what was fleeting yet vivid. To do this, he must use a form of representation, and, because he is a painter, he will use a visual image. He will try to create a set of visual relationships on a flat, static surface that will adumbrate his experience with the character of that small Kansas town.

The options available to him are as numerous as the techniques at his command and his inventiveness in using them. What he is able to say about his experience in that town will be influenced by a multiplicity of factors that come into play as he puts brush to canvas: his concentration on certain aspects of the town, the technical skills at his disposal, the limits to which the paint will yield to his desires, and the extent to which he will yield to its demands. Ultimately, however, the task is one of representing his experience with a place. It is one of creating a publicly shareable image that will deliver to the competent eye an experience worth having.[1]

The decision to use paint as material and the visual image as medium for conveying his experience is, technically speaking, one of several options available. The town might have been rendered in dance, through drama, in poetry, or in prose. But for a painter the choice is obvious: an image made from paint and applied to a stretched canvas. For him, one might say, there is no choice. He does what he knows how to do. In fact, even his experience was shaped by his expressive skills, while, at the same time, the use of his expressive skills is guided by his experience.

Had our traveler been not a painter but a composer, the task would also have been one of image making,[2] but the form of representation would have been auditory rather than visual. The composer's task is to say about that town what can be said through music.

Suppose our traveler was neither a painter nor a composer, but a sociologist. Surely what is experienced would be influenced by what the sociologist knows how to do. It is likely that her conception of the town would be shaped by the sociological categories she knows. What the sociologist "asks for" will profoundly influence the nature of the answers she receives. Thus, whenever a form of representation is used (in this case sociological prose), there is a concomitant neglect of those qualities of the world that the form cannot "name." Neglect, in the case of our sociological traveler, should not be regarded as something unique to sociology. *Every* form of representation neglects some aspect of the world.[3] Just as perception itself must be selective in order to focus, so, too, must be the content that a form of representation can contain. Not everything can be said through anything. The selection of a form of representation is a selection of what can be used to transform a private experience into a public one. Forms of representation that will not take the impress of particular kinds of experience cannot, by definition, be used to convey them.

The selection of a form of representation not only functions as a vehicle for conveying what has been conceptualized, it also helps articulate conceptual forms. Consider an example from drawing. If one knows that one were going to draw, say, the diner in the town in Kansas, the character and the detail of the diner are likely to be looked for, seen, and remembered in a way that is much more intense, detailed, and vivid than if one were going to compose a piece of music about it or to describe it through the prose of sociology. The demands of the task guide one's perception. What one cannot see or imagine, one cannot draw.

Thus, it is possible to identify the several ways in which the selection of a form of representation influences not only the content of representation but the content of conception as well. First, as one becomes skilled in the use of particular forms of representation, the tendency to want to use such forms increases, and the focus that they engender is likely to become a salient frame of reference for perception.[4] The kinds of nets we know how to weave determine the kinds of nets we cast. These nets, in turn, determine the kinds of fish we catch. Second, the skills we possess in the use of particular forms of representation influence the extent to which what we know conceptually can be represented publicly. Someone who cannot sing might be able to compose great melodies, but they are not likely to be represented by him through song. The degree to which skills are absent or technique is weak is the degree to which forms of representation are themselves weakened. Indeed, skill is regarded so highly by Olson (1978) that he considers intelligence itself to be "skill

in a medium." Third, the particular form of representation one selects places constraints upon what one is able to say, regardless of
the level of skill one possesses or the variety of techniques one knows
how to use. Some aspects of human experience are simply better
expressed through some forms than through others. If it were possible to convey everything that humans wanted to convey with one or
two forms of representation, the others would be redundant.

Consider, for example, the experience of suspense and how it
might be portrayed through two different forms of representation,
music and visual art. It is not difficult to imagine how that quality of
experience we call suspense might be represented in music. As a
matter of fact, it is likely that most readers can readily imagine the
kind of music they might compose, even as they read these words.
The image of the chase in old cowboy movies or the scores of old
"who-dun-it" films come readily to mind. Because suspense is
largely a temporal experience, music, which is also temporal, is an
appropriate vehicle for representing it.[5]

But now try to imagine how suspense might be represented
through a visual image. Here the task becomes considerably more
difficult. Aside from some trite illustrations, it is very difficult to even
conceive of, let alone paint or sculpt, a visual representation of such
an experience. Visual images are more spatial than temporal; suspense is more temporal than spatial. The two are difficult to reconcile.
The examples that one could provide are numerous, but the point
remains the same. *The choice of a form of representation is a choice in the
way the world will be conceived, as well as choice in the way it will be
publicly represented.*

Perhaps one last example is in order. Assume that, for some
reason, the only form of representation we were allowed to use during a period of time was mathematics. Suppose, further, that during
that period we thought of something quite humorous that we wanted
to share with others. How might we use mathematics to express
humor? How could we quip or be funny through addition or subtrac-
tion, calculus, geometry or algebra? To suggest that mathematics is
difficult to use for representing humor is not to imply that it is not
extremely useful for other things. Mathematics, like every other form
of representation, is an appropriate vehicle for expressing some aspects of human consciousness, but not all aspects. To be restricted to
it alone would eventually not only limit expression, but put the
brakes on conception as well.

Thus far, I have spoken of the use of forms of representation as
though the direction of the activity was from conception to expres-

sion, from what is conceived to its transformation through a form of representation into a public image. While the process often does move in this direction, by no means is this the only way in which it can proceed. No one working with a material, whether words or other qualities, conceptualizes every detail prior to action. The process of working with material is, among other things, a heuristic process. Through it ideas are formed, negotiated, revised, discovered (Collingwood, 1958). The course of inquiry seldom follows the path of an arrow. Indeed, some artists intentionally work in a way that fosters the adventitious, almost intuitively exemplifying the truth of Aristotle's observation that "art loves chance."[6] Rather than trying to impose a preconceived image upon a material, their aim is to act and, from the action, to leave tracks, as it were, of where they have been. One such group was the abstract expressionists of whom the noted art critic Harold Rosenberg (1965) wrote:

> At a certain moment the canvas began to appear to one American painter after another as an arena in which to act—rather than a space in which to reproduce, redesign, analyze or "express" an object, actual or imagined. What was to go on the canvas was not a picture but an event.
>
> The painter no longer approached his easel with an image in his mind; he went up to it with material in front of him. The image would be the result of this encounter. (p. 25)

For many artists the process is a matter of qualitative negotiation. Although the work might have been initiated as a desire to impose a concept upon pliable material, the work itself gradually begins to "participate" in the negotiations. Gradually the work "tells" the artist what is needed. What may have been begun as a lecture becomes a conversation. What may have been started as a monologue becomes a dialogue.

It should not be surprising that the process itself yields ideas that were not a part of the initiating conception. Working within forms of representation provides the individual with an opportunity not only to perform in the role of maker but in the role of critic as well. The actions one takes and the ideas one expresses are stabilized in the medium in which one works: one hears the music one plays, one reads the words one writes, one sees the images one creates (Gardner, 1973). Each of these stabilized public forms provides a content for analysis, revision, and appreciation. The first critic of an individual's efforts is the maker himself.

Perhaps nowhere is the critical function more obvious—though it exists in equal degree in other forms of representation—than it is in writing. The first drafts that one produces are almost always riddled with ambiguities, uncertainties, lapses of logic, inconsistencies, errors in grammar, and the like. The creation of prose allows the editing process to proceed, to detect errors of omission and commission. In short, the written form makes it possible to refine thinking and to clarify meaning.

The opportunity to use a form of representation can generate ideas in at least two ways. First, the opportunity to act upon a material itself motivates one to think. Countless ideas are developed because of a need to present a paper at a professional meeting or to meet a deadline set by others. The demands of the occasion motivate the creation.

Second, as already indicated, the work to be produced is never wholly conceived prior to action. The process of working with a form of representation clarifies, confers detail, provides material upon which ideas can be worked out and corrections made.

Because different forms of representation emphasize the use of different sensory systems, the kinds of psychological processes they evoke are also likely to differ. We might well ask what this means for the development of cognition. If the kinds of mental skills or forms of intelligence one possesses are influenced by opportunities to use them, does it not seem likely that the forms of representation children have access to or are encouraged to use will shape the mental skills or forms of intelligence they will be able to develop? (Cole, 1974). If, furthermore, the kinds of meaning that individuals secure are related to the kinds of concepts they form and if different forms of representation tend to stimulate the formulation of different concepts, what does unequal emphasis on forms of representation mean for what people will come to know? When Basil Bernstein (1971) writes that the curriculum is a device not only for conveying the past but also for shaping consciousness, this is, I believe, what he had in mind. When we define the curriculum, we are also defining the opportunities the young will have to experience different forms of consciousness. To have a musical consciousness, one must interact with music. To have a visual artistic consciousness, one must interact with visual art. To experience the poetics of language, poetry must be available. But the argument goes even further.

Humans appear to have a *need* to shift the forms of consciousness they experience. Even under the most difficult circumstances, when people lived at the edge of survival, they decorated their pots, inscribed their utensils, danced, and created images that allowed their experience to vary. To know a set of conditions other than what they had known, images other than those they had typically encountered were created, often ingeniously. In this respect, one might regard forms of representation as mind-altering devices, as vehicles through which the quality of experience is changed.

This view seems to me to be consistent with the way in which we lead our lives. We go to films, plays, and concerts; read history; and visit galleries and museums to have experiences that only such activities are likely to make possible. The experience, when it is successful, is mind altering. We come away refreshed, feeling better, sometimes even nourished by our break from routine and the forms of consciousness that dominate it. In this sense, variety contributes to our mental health.

Thus far, I have provided only a general definition of forms of representation. Perhaps it is time to be more specific.

A Closer Look at Forms of Representation

I use the phrase *form of representation* to refer to the expressive medium used to make a conception public. Any form of representation one elects to use must convey information through its appeal to one or more of the sensory systems. Hence, a form of representation may be visual, auditory, tactile, kinesthetic, gustatory, or olfactory. It is obvious that in film, for example, forms of representation used are not only visual but auditory. It is obvious, also, that in dance forms of representation are not only visual and auditory but also kinesthetic. Speech conveys not only by "pointing to" referents that are visual, but also by its melody and cadence—auditory qualities that are central aspects of the message. Thus, forms of representation often combine and interact in the way in which they carry information forward.

In deciding to conceptualize "forms of representation" in terms of its expressive medium, I considered and rejected other alternatives. Music or the visual arts, for example, could have been identified as forms of representation. Yet to conceptualize the term at this level of abstraction is to construct a virtually endless list of categories. I prefer, therefore, to regard the nature of the vehicle as a form of representation, rather than particular culturally defined means such as painting, music, dance, poetry, film. This means, of course, that in many of these vehicles several forms of representation will be used.

I also considered regarding a discipline such as philosophy, biology, history, sociology, or psychology as a form of representation. This, too, was rejected. The reason is that, although different disciplines use different terms and methods, all the social sciences, for example, are couched in propositional language, and, from that standpoint, the expressive medium they use to represent conceptions does not differ. Thus, overall, it appeared to me much more conceptually neat to define ''form of representation'' in relation to the nature of the expressive medium and thus to underscore the fact that the kinds of meanings we are able to secure depend in large measure on the varieties of sensory information we can experience. Forms of representation are a major source of such experience.

Figure 3.1 presents schematically the relationships that hold between the various elements described thus far. At the center of the figure is a sentient individual possessing a sensory system, a personal history of prior learning, a set of attitudes or dispositions to focus in particular ways, and a set of representational skills. The individual transacts with an environment in which a variety of qualities are present. Out of this transaction, depending upon the individual's attitudes, purposes, and prior learning, aspects of that environment are construed and concepts formed. These concepts are formed out

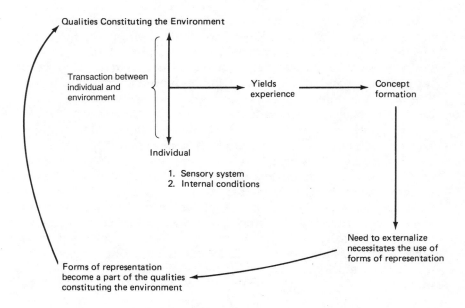

FIGURE 3.1. Transactions Between the Individual and the Environment

of the experience that the sensory system makes possible. They may subsequently be labeled through the use of discourse, although much of our experience will not take the impress of a verbal label. The kind of meaning the individual is likely to secure through transaction with the qualities of the environment will depend upon the kinds of concepts he or she has formed, that is, it will depend upon the character of the qualities the individual has selected and experienced.

If the individual wishes to express the meanings secured from the transactions with those qualities, he or she must use some form of representation to do so. The particular form of representation chosen will be influenced by his or her skills as well as purposes. Once the individual makes the transformation from the conception to the representation, the qualities created in these represented forms become a part of the environment upon which he or she can reflect further. The creation of new environmental qualities through the use of a form of representation makes the editing process possible, which, in turn, makes it possible to revise, correct, and strengthen the ideas expressed through the form chosen. Thus, a form of representation serves not only as a means for conveying to others conceptions held by an individual; it also provides feedback for the individual.

Because the kind of experience an individual has depends upon the kinds of qualities the sensory system picks up and because meaning depends upon experience, the character and distribution of qualities in an environment and the particular focus an individual brings to that environment affect the kind of meaning he or she is likely to have. Because particular forms of representation often tend to emphasize particular qualities and utilize a particular sensory system, the kind of meaning that a single form of representation can express is limited. When the skills necessary for using a form of representation are not available or the encouragement to use them is not provided, the kinds of meanings that an individual might secure from such forms are likely to be forgone. For example, children who are given no opportunity to compose music are unlikely to secure the meanings that the creation of music makes possible. Nor are they likely to regard the world in a way relevant to the creation of a musical equivalent.

It is important to reemphasize that the relationship between the individual and the environment is a transactive one. By this I mean that both the qualities of the environment *and* the individual's internal conditions affect the kind of experience or kinds of concepts that will be created. It is simply not the case that the qualities themselves determine what will be selected; nor is it the case that the individual will entirely project his or her internal conditions on the environment. There is a give-and-take in the process. Each factor makes its own contribution, and out of the transaction experience is born. This point is particularly germane for designers of curriculum.

Teachers and curriculum designers have no direct access to the internal conditions of the individual except through the qualities they create in the environment. Owners of expensive restaurants, people in the advertising industry, costume designers, and the like have long known of the importance of image. Although experience cannot be controlled or determined, it can be influenced by the conditions with which an individual interacts. What is true of the advertising industry is also true of the schools. The difference resides within their respective aims. The advertiser's aim is to manipulate the individual's behavior so that it affords a profit to the advertiser's client. Prediction of consumer performance is a virtue; critical choice is a vice. In education, critical choice is a virtue; merely the successful manipulation of student behavior is a vice. What we seek in education is the cultivation of intelligence in the variety of forms in which it can operate. We seek to liberate rather than to control.

Modes of Treating Forms of Representation

The conceptualization of forms of representation as vehicles through which conceptions are externalized does not, by itself, describe the particular ways in which such forms can be treated. Given any form of representation, say one that is visual or linguistic, how might it be treated so that it represents what someone is attempting to convey? To describe these ways of creating "equivalents," the term *modes of treatment* has been formulated. Any form of representation can be treated in one or more of three modes: mimetic, expressive, and conventional.

The *mimetic mode* conveys through imitation, that is, it represents by replicating within the limits of the medium employed the surface features of some aspect of the qualitative world. There are, throughout human history, numerous examples of how mimetic modes of treatment function, from the use of hieroglyphics and pictographs that were employed to imitate the basic structural features of the visual world to the most advanced forms of photography and holography. Just what is it that mimetic modes of treatment do? Simply stated, they extract the salient features of some aspect of the world

and represent them as an image within some medium. They repro-
duce, to use Rudolf Arnheim's phrase, the structural equivalent of
the features of world as experienced (1954; see especially chapter 4).

The images of animals drawn on the walls of the Lescaux caves
were probably the result of early humans' interest in representing
their observations of the world. It seems reasonable to assume that
members of the community knew what they were intended to describe through their visual correspondence to their referents. In the
use of hieroglyphics we have not only the abstracted visual representation of human figures, animals, furniture, and so forth, but we
have them in a time sequence, a visual narrative that individuals are
able to read. Hieroglyphics exemplify the human ability to combine
both spatial experience (the visual image) and temporal experience
by sequencing visual images in a form that not only parallels the
visual experience at a particular point in time but over time as well
(Gregory, 1966).

If we look at a more modern example of the ways in which
mimetic modes of treatment occur, it is vividly apparent in the use of
highway signs. Particularly in Europe one will find signs that tell the
driver what he or she can expect to encounter as the car moves down
the highway: a curve in the road, a dip, animals crossing, zigzags,
castles nearby, turn offs, and so forth. In each case, the image created
shares some structural similarity with the object or situation it is
designed to represent. Even though the form of representation is
highly schematized, it presents the driver with as much information
as needed—and probably as much as can be handled at seventy miles
per hour.

Consider also paintings and photographs. Suppose you wanted
to know what the south of France looked like, or Chartres Cathedral,
or your long-lost cousin Beatrice. You could, of course, read descriptions of them and perhaps, if the writer were very skilled, it might be
possible to gain a fairly good idea of their features. But a photograph
or a painting will usually do the job much better. Their special features are more likely to be represented in a form that displays their
characteristics through a form of representation that is itself spatial
than through one that is not. If we are trying to find someone disem-
barking from an airplane whom we have never met before, we would
probably do better if we had a photograph than if we had a verbal
description or a set of numbers describing the person's height and
weight.

Perhaps the most telling example of the mimetic mode of treating
visual forms of representation is to be found in the use of finger-

prints. Here what one has is a direct visual imprint of a textured surface. The prints duplicate in virtually every detail the configurations of the surface of the fingers. Indeed, the correspondence is so close that among several million examples of prints on file in the FBI offices in Washington, no two are identical. One print is structurally isomorphic with the finger of a particular individual.

Given the utility of mimesis, it is curious to me to encounter Nelson Goodman's (1968) assertion that "A Constable painting of Marlboro Castle is more like any other picture than it is like the castle" or that "None of the automobiles off an assembly line is a picture of the rest" (p. 5). I find these statements curious because we do, in fact, expect a painting of Marlboro Castle to represent, that is to say, to look like the subject. If it does not, we are disappointed. And if we go into an automobile showroom, select a car and ask the salesman to order the same car, except in a different color, we are in fact using the car on the showroom floor as a model that we expect our car, when delivered, to duplicate. If we find that another model has arrived instead, or that the grill has been altered, or that another motor has been installed, or that different tires have been affixed, we have cause not only for complaint but also for canceling our order. A painting of Marlboro Castle looks more like any other painting than the castle itself *only* if we choose to disregard its image and pay attention to the paint, canvas, stretcher, and frame.

Or consider still another example, the use of a prototype in the production of automobiles. It is standard practice to build prototype automobiles that in every respect are to be reproduced on the assembly line. Cars coming off the line duplicate these prototypes, which themselves are representations of designers, and engineers, conceptions. When a car coming off the line does not possess the features of the prototype, there is (or should be) a callback: something has gone amiss.

What such practices exemplify are efforts at mimesis, the prototypical model being the standard against which other cars coming off the line are to be appraised. In this way, as well as through the pictures and specifications provided in sales brochures, a mimetic function is performed. Like the highway signs, the prototype describes what is to be found when the journey is completed. It "pictures" in detail, ideally. as a perfect replica, what workers, buyers, and management are to find when the work has been completed. In this sense, one car does indeed stand for another.

Now it is true that in some respects a painting of a car is more like any other painting or car than it is like a person or like some other thing. But that is true only if we shift context and disregard the function of representation. A scientific formula—H_2O—is more like any other formula—CO_2—than it is like water. We can always, I suppose, choose to disregard the intended function of a form in order to attend to another, and for some purposes such disregard might be functional. But Goodman's argument that imitation is largely irrelevant to representation is, I believe, unsound. Humans have for thousands of years represented through mimesis. Indeed, techniques such as perspective were invented to make more credible the representations attempted (Gombrich, 1969). This is not to say that paintings or even photographs are simply copies in the same way that fingerprints or death masks are copies. Idiosyncratic expression and interpretation are always present, at least to some degree. It is to say that we have learned how to read schematized images and that, for a great many kinds of information, we do not require the degree of mimesis that fingerprints provide.

Most of the examples I have used thus far are visual, but mimesis occurs in other forms of representation as well. Auditory forms of representation, such as music, can be composed to imitate the sound of thunder, running brooks, riders on horseback, and so forth. Words can be onomatopoeic. Tactile forms can be created to imitate a wide range of other tactile qualities, and so forth. The point here is that the imitation of selected features of the phenomenal world through an empirically available material has been and is one of the major means through which representation is achieved.

There is another point about the mimetic mode of treatment that is so obvious that it is often neglected. That is, for the purposes of mimesis, the closer the form of representation is to the content represented, the closer the mimesis is likely to be. Thus, to represent what is visual, forms of representation that provide visual information are, in general, likely to be more revealing than forms that provide other kinds of information. To know how something sounds, forms of representation that emphasize the auditory are more appropriate than forms that emphasize the visual. To know what someone said, a duplication of the words is more appropriate than a picture. This is not to suggest that transformations of experience from one sense modality to representation in forms that emphasize another should not or do not occur. Such a suggestion would mean the demise of literature. It is to suggest that mimetic functions tend to operate most successfully when the sense modality emphasized in the form of representation is like that which it aims to represent.

Allow me one further observation. In many situations the meaning of an experience is not simply the function of the experience secured through one of the senses, but, rather, of the interaction among the "data" picked up by the several senses. Consider discourse. When people talk, the meanings conveyed do not simply rely on what is said but on how it is said as well: the intonation and emphasis people give to the words they use, the gestures they make while speaking, their expression, the context in which what they have to say is said, what preceded in the conversation, and so forth. The absence of such features in transcripts of discourse can radically alter the meanings that, in fact, were conveyed when the discourse occurred.[7] To pick up the varieties of information that accompany the discourse itself—if, indeed, one can talk about the "discourse itself," since it is never by itself—a variety of sensory systems must operate, and one must know how to read the meanings that the content they make possible provides. The ability to reconstruct varieties of information through sound and sight, tempo and context, is one of the virtues of film. Perhaps that is one of the reasons why film is so captivating and compelling.

A second kind of treatment used to shape forms of representation is the *expressive mode*. By expressive, I mean that what is represented is not the surface features of the object or event, but, rather, its deep structure or, in other words, its expressive character. Consider the movement of a jet airplane speeding down a runway about to take off. The plane moves along very slowly and gradually increases its speed. Its speed continues to increase, and about three-quarters of the way down the runway, its nose rises, and, like a duck leaving a lake, it lifts off the surface of the earth. Such an experience, if we were standing on the observation deck of an airport building, would be auditory as well as visual. We would experience a stark white form accelerating and gradually becoming nothing more than a small dark speck against the vast expansive blue sky. It is this movement—this gentle, graceful takeoff, the sound of the jet engines gradually diminishing in volume, the plane shrinking in size as it moves into the sky—that a dancer or a graphic artist might create. Such creations have little to do with the imitation of surface features, but much more to do with the experiences of acceleration and of a slow rise into the atmosphere. How these expressive qualities might be represented is precisely what the artist must determine. There are no codified formulas for producing them. What the artist wants to do is not to imitate the surface features of a moving plane, but to reveal its essential properties, that is to say, its expressive character. Here, too, a kind of imitation is at work, but it is not imitation of things seen.

Rather, it is an imitation of things felt. The form of representation is treated expressively rather than mimetically. The analogic relationship is not established through the imitation of appearance, but through the creation of a form that generates the expressiveness of slowly accelerating movement.

Why have artists been interested in such tasks? Why should such efforts occupy a central place in the history of the arts? At least a part of the reason is because much of what is most important in human experience is not what is apparent, but, instead, what is felt about what is apparent. Things are not always what they appear to be on the surface. They need to be seen in terms of the kind of emotional life that they generate. The sense of curiosity displayed by a very young child exploring a new toy or the fear of an old man anticipating imminent death are not simply physical movements. Such configurations possess a pervasive quality that conveys to the sensitive perceiver the character of curiosity and fear. Expressive forms must penetrate the surface features. Just how such forms, whether human or not, can convey such qualities of life is not altogether clear. Gestalt and associationist theories of meaning hold competing views, but it is not necessary to explain these theoretical views here. What is important is to recognize that the expressive treatment of forms of representation does occur and does function to shape our experience.

If to know about the character of life in a school or classroom or a suburb or ghetto requires one to know not only about surface appearance but also about the character of life within, then it is imperative that those who wish to make such knowledge public use means that can convey the qualities they seek to express. It is here that expressive modes of treatment are crucial. In literature and in poetry artistic achievement is realized in the expressive character of the forms created, not because such forms are necessarily beautiful or pleasant but because, without them, the very content that the artist wishes to convey could not be expressed. The expressive mode of treatment is, therefore, not simply a pleasant affectation, a dressing up of content to make it more palatable; it is itself part and parcel of the content of the form of representation. When descriptions of emotionally loaded situations lack the emotionality that they hold for those who live in those situations, a significant kind of bias and distortion results. To use a form to represent life in the concentration camps at Buchenwald or Dachau that omits the character of life as experienced by the inmates is to render less than a partial view of those camps; it is to mislead.

A third type of treatment is the *conventional mode*. By conventional, I simply mean that, as individuals are socialized within a culture, they learn that certain conventions stand in the place of something else. A red light, a cross, the word *table*, the flag, the almost wholly arbitrary vocabulary of our discursive language are examples of the conventional mode of treating forms of representation. Words and colors are neither mimetic (although at one time they might have been) nor expressive (although they might be used expressively as words are used in literature and in poetry). The relationship between the form and referent is arbitrary. *Pain* in English means something like a sharp, uncomfortable feeling, while in French it means bread. There is nothing in the word per se to commend it to one rather than to the other referent. What matters is that, within each culture, there is agreement among those who use the word concerning the referent. This is not to suggest that meanings, even those related to convention, lack variability in interpretation by different individuals. The range of the variance is far narrower, however, than it is in either of the other two modes of treatment.

There is, of course, an important and interesting difference between the mimetic and the expressive modes of treatment and the conventional mode. In both the mimetic and the expressive modes, analogic relationships operate. In each case what is created parallels some aspect of the form being represented. In the conventional mode of treatment, this is not the case. A table does not look like how it sounds. For a word or a sentence to have meaning, the individual must be able to imagine the referent for the term or terms employed. This does not mean that, for every word used, there is a corresponding image. We have so mastered discourse that we do not need to conjure up an image in order to speak or write. If we encounter a word whose referent we cannot imagine, however, we can have no conception of what it means. It is in this sense that language functions as a surrogate for an image. If the surrogate is to have meaning, we must be able to conceive of its referent, even when the referent is a so-called abstract category. This is why, when children do not understand a word, we try to help them by providing examples.[8]

The distinctions I have made between the mimetic, the expressive, and the conventional should not be taken to mean that a form of representation uses only one mode of treatment. The three are often combined. For example, much visual art, particularly painting, uses mimetic, expressive, and conventional elements within the same work. Literature and poetry exemplify the mimetic mode in the way in which the sounds of events are emulated, the expressive mode in the way in which the structure of the prose penetrates the surface features of the events portrayed, and the conventional mode through the standardized use of language and symbol.

But perhaps the most vivid example of a vehicle that combines varieties of representation and modes of treatment is to be found in film. The modern film not only lets us see how something looks or sounds, but, when artistically successful, it also enables us to experience the underlying structure of the event and places portrayed. Films such as *A River Runs Through It* make it possible for the moviegoer to get a sense of what life was like in Montana in the 1920s. It invites one into an expansive environment permeated by nature, in which a passion for the perfection of fly casting becomes as dramatic an enterprise as a Greek drama. Here we encounter people who allow us to grasp their unique temperaments, their driving ambitions, and their most deeply held values. We come to understand a quality of life that for most Americans is long gone. *A River Runs Through It*, like most powerful films, exploits the mimetic, the expressive, and the conventional to make insight born of feeling possible. Through insight, feeling follows. Robert Redford, the director and producer of *A River Runs Through It*, has created a film that furthers our understanding of both past and present; the issues of the 1920s are not absent in the 1990s. He achieves this through his artistic treatment of a combination of forms that is, in many ways, most acutely presented in the most powerful of twentieth-century art forms, the movie.

The Syntaxes of Forms of Representation

Thus far I have spoken of forms of representation and modes of treatment. The former are those vehicles human beings have invented to make public privately experienced conceptions. The latter are the means used to shape the forms used to express a conception. Thus auditory forms of representation such as music can be treated mimetically as in the musical imitation of a man on horseback, expressively as in romantic music, or conventionally as in music that has specifically been assigned conventional meaning—"God Save the Queen," for example. The way forms of representation are treated does not, however, reveal much about the manner in which the components within a form of representation are related. It is to that topic that we now turn.

All forms of representation are forms arranged. I refer to these arrangements of forms as *syntax*. The term *syntax* is most commonly used in relation to spoken or written language, but its root, which in

Latin is *syntaxis,* means "to arrange." Syntax is an arrangement of parts within a whole. In the arts, for example, a variety of terms relate to the problem of putting or arranging elements into a coherent structure. In music, composers and arrangers work with auditory elements; in the visual arts, painters determine the composition of visual elements; in architecture, architects arrange spaces. There are similar arrangements in dance, as well as in prose and poetry. Thus the term *syntax* need not be limited to discourse, whether spoken or written. It can, and originally did, refer to the more general problem of arranging elements within a whole.

If we examine the basis upon which elements are related within various forms of representation, it becomes clear that a continuum can be formulated on which it is possible to place individual forms of representation. At one end of the continuum are those forms of representation whose elements must be arranged according to a publicly codified set of rules. To use the elements within a form of representation skillfully, one must know the rules related to that form and how to use them. Consider simple arithmetic as an example. A specific rule or convention must be followed without deviation if arithmetic problems are to be dealt with correctly. A great deal of attention, particularly during early schooling, is devoted to helping children learn how to follow the rules in order to compute correctly. Similar rules hold for grammar, spelling, and punctuation. Although there is more leeway in the use of these forms for personal judgment, they are essentially *rule governed.* Learning to speak and write grammatically, like learning to spell and compute correctly, means, in part, learning how to follow codified rules. Indeed, it is precisely because the rules are codified and public that the skills related to their correct use are, compared to tasks where no comparable rules exist, relatively easy to teach and to evaluate. And this is why it is possible to say of a child's performance, when the child employs a form using a rule-governed syntax, that the answers are correct or incorrect. Such conclusions are impossible to draw in appraising the child's performance related to poetry, dance, music, or visual art.

At the other end of the continuum are those forms of representation that use a syntax that is more *figurative* than rule governed. The forms of representation about which I speak are exemplified, but not exhausted, by the fine arts, free verse, and literature. What the arts make possible—indeed, what they tend to elicit from those who use them—is an invitation to invent novel ways to combine elements. One of the reasons why form changes so rapidly in the arts, as compared to arithmetic, spelling, grammar, and punctuation, is because a premium is placed on productive novelty in the arts, ingenuity is considered a virtue. In spelling, it is considered a vice.

In saying, as I have, that the arts are not highly rule governed, I do not mean to imply that artistic conventions and social expectations do not influence what artists create. An artist wishing to produce a surrealist or op art painting fully understands that certain forms invented in the past will need to be reproduced by the artist in the present. A composer wishing to create a romantic symphony will feel a need to adhere to the formal structure of music created by romantic composers of the nineteenth century. In a sense, the "rules" are embedded in previous work. Anyone who wishes to produce similar work must observe those "rules."

But such "rules," if that is what they should be called, are not formally codified as they are for arithmetic, spelling, and punctuation. They are nowhere near as prescriptive in character, and they do not lead, as they do in spelling and arithmetic, to uniform solutions to common tasks or problems. A group of children given the same problem in arithmetic will, if they know the operations required, produce the same responses that, without ambiguity, can be judged correct or incorrect. Children asked to create a surrealist painting or a romantic melody will not be expected to and cannot in fact create identical solutions. The less rule-governed and more figurative the syntax, the more it permits idiosyncratic interpretation and novelty in form. Or, to put it another way, the further one moves away from conventional prescription, the more scope one has for personal choice. Thus, it is not surprising that the arts should be commonly regarded as providing optimal opportunity for personal expression for cultivating creativity and for encouraging individuality. What has been recognized intuitively is that the arts are forms that are not restricted to highly formalized rules. There is no such thing as an "incorrect" poem.

The distinction that I have made between syntaxes that are rule governed and those that are figurative might appear to be wrong headed. After all, is not every painter or composer guided by rules that, when followed, lead to the creation of a form reflective of some artistic style, be it baroque, cubist, surrealist, or some other? And are not such styles the result of following the rules? A painter who wants to create an early cubist painting must obey the rules of early cubism: a restricted range of colors will be used, the surface features of an object will be broken into planes, the sides and back of an object will be seen as well as the front, and so forth. Is not learning how to paint or to compose or to write in a particular style the result of learning rules that are, in a sense, embodied within the style itself? If this is the case, then why differentiate between the rule governed and the figurative, even by degree?

There are several reasons for the distinction. In the first place, no painting or musical composition, no dance or poem is governed by rules wherein each element and combination among them is so specified that, by applying the rules to the performance or object made, one can without ambiguity determine if the performance or object is correct or incorrect. Although a sonnet by convention must have fourteen lines, no more and no less, what is artistically significant about a sonnet is not its fourteen lines but how and what it conveys. No rules can be applied for making this determination. Likewise, while an early cubist painter will use a restrictive range of colors and will break up forms into a series of planes, what makes the painting a work of art is not the fact that it follows those rules but that it generates a certain quality of experience in those who look at it in a competent way. For that achievement, there are no rules.

A second consideration is that, in rule-governed syntaxes, literal paraphrase is possible. One can translate the content of one form or statement into another without loss of meaning. The statement 85 plus 35 equals 120 means exactly what 35 plus 85 means, or 100 plus 20, or any other sum that equals 120. Because the rules of transformation are explicit, we can move from one formulation to another without losing information. There is no comparable translatability in forms of representation that emphasize figurative syntaxes. The form as a whole embodies its meaning. The relationships among its "parts" are unique configurations, and when change is made in a "part," the meaning conveyed through the whole also changes. Furthermore, no codified set of rules can be applied in order to recover such meaning. Meaning depends upon judgment. The use of critical intelligence is a necessity. In short, one might say that syntaxes that are rule governed are codes; those that are figurative are metaphors. The rules for decoding codes are specific and public; for explaining metaphors, imagination is required.

Syntaxes at each end of the continuum, from rule governed to figurative, have different virtues. Rule-governed syntaxes increase the possibility of consensus or, in statistical terms, interjudge agreement. By specifying the rules to be applied to the elements within a form of representation, it is possible for anyone who knows the rules and their application to determine with a high degree of accuracy whether or not the operations have been performed correctly. In areas of human performance where personal choice or idiosyncratic interpretation or behavior is a liability—working on an assembly line, for example—it is extremely useful to work with forms of representation having a syntax whose use does not require imagination or even depend upon human judgment. In such situations, what one seeks is the correct application of a standard (Dewey, 1934/1958; see especially Chapter 13). It becomes increasingly possible, as one uses forms of representation whose syntaxes are located at the rule-governed end of the continuum, to speak of correct or incorrect solutions or answers. As one moves toward the figurative end of the continuum, the terms *correct* and *incorrect* become increasingly inappropriate. What one might say about such solutions is that some are better or worse than others. It is here that deliberation and judgment become crucial, and it is in syntaxes operating at this end of the continuum that complex higher mental processes come into play.[9] The security of knowing when one is right or wrong is sacrificed for the uncertainty and fallibility that human judgment necessarily yields.

It is important to note that the almost exclusive emphasis in the elementary school curricula is on mastering forms of representation that emphasize rule-governed syntaxes. There may be several reasons for this. Probably the most important is that mastery of cultural conventions such as reading, writing, and arithmetic have an enormously important instrumental value. Without the ability to perform the operations these forms require, a student is handicapped as he or she advances in school. But it is perhaps even more important that the child's ability to deal with messages from the culture at large not be severely impeded. It is clear that skill in the use of written and verbal language exceeds simple forms of rote learning. Interpretation is always to some degree necessary. Yet, at the elementary level, the emphasis is largely on learning the rules, knowing the correct ways to form letters, to spell, to punctuate, and to employ grammar. The rules of basic arithmetic operations are to be learned until they become rote; the less one has to think about how they are to be used, the better. Speed in the completion of arithmetic problems is one index of mastery since the more one has to think, the less one has mastered the rules.

Within the context of schools, mastery of the three Rs is a necessary condition for dealing with many other subjects the child will encounter, virtually all of which emphasize rule-governed syntaxes and place a premium on conventional modes of treatment. As they are typically taught, science, social studies, and geography tend to lean toward the rule-governed end of the continuum and employ conventionalized terms that the student must learn.

This prescriptiveness in curriculum, particularly at the early grades, may be emphasized for still other reasons. Because the rules of writing, reading, and arithmetic are public and codified, the tasks of teaching and evaluating student performance are made easier. In the typical math curriculum the teacher knows what problems are to be assigned, knows the specific operations the child needs to know in order to do these problems, and knows what counts as a correct solution. There is, compared to the teaching of literature, music, or art, little ambiguity about content, method, or conclusion. The textbook defines each; indeed, materials are available that allow students as well as teachers to "look up" the correct answer to each of the problems encountered.

One might well ask about the concomitant learning that goes on at school when the emphasis in curriculum is on forms of representation that emphasize rule-governed syntaxes and conventional modes of treatment. It seems quite likely that one of the things that children learn from a curriculum of this kind is that for every problem there is a correct solution. Furthermore, the teacher not only knows the solution, but knows what methods are to be used to achieve it. The child's problem becomes largely one of learning how to follow rules and to complete assignments—in short, to learn how to do what is expected by others who know what the correct solutions are to the problems students encounter in school.

Now there is an appropriate sense in which teachers do know—indeed, they ought to know—what the answers are to the problems they set for students. I am not suggesting that there be cognitive parity between child and teacher. I am speaking of emphasis, of tone, of the pervasive quality of classroom life, and, most of all, of the need to understand what we neglect cultivating in classrooms—what I have called the "null curriculum" (Eisner, 1985). Being educationally rigorous does not necessarily require going back several decades to dredge up mindless methods of teaching, rote forms of student performance, and docile obedience to the will of authority. Going back to the so-called basics is not good enough. Cognition is wider than the forms of representation that are common to propositional discourse and simple forms of arithmetic. To apply such solutions to the problems of improving the quality of education is to underestimate seriously the intellectual capacities children possess. How can such intellectual capacities be tapped? How can educational evaluation capture what is educationally significant about classroom life? It is toward a wider view of curriculum and evaluation that we turn next.

4 From Cognition to Curriculum

The previous chapters of this book were designed to advance a conception of the role of the senses in concept formation and to describe the forms of representation that humans employ to give public status to those concepts. I have argued that the senses are primary information pickup systems; they are the means through which information is constructed from the "blooming, buzzing confusion" that William James (1890, p. 448) has said we all inhabit. The processes of selection, organization, recall, and imagination that transform sensory data into information would have little social significance if the public display of our conceptual life did not occur. Representation, never complete or isomorphic with the images that constitute our concepts, provides the means for making this transformation of the private to the public.

The educational meanings of the conceptions I have described achieve their practical import as they affect what teachers and students do in their shared educational lives. Ideas about human learning or perception that do not influence classroom practice have little "cash value" from an educational perspective. The task then is to transform ideas into practice and to test these ideas in schools and in classrooms. There are two major areas where these ideas can be tested. The first is the curriculum: the program of activities and opportunities provided to the young. The second resides in the artistry with which that program is mediated by teachers. We call such artistry "teaching."

If different forms of representation make different kinds of meaning possible, what kinds of meanings do students secure when those forms are used in school programs? If students need to acquire different kinds of "literacies" in order to construe meanings from these forms, how can such literacies be developed? If teachers are to use such forms of representation to teach a subject—say, mathematics or history—just what kind of teaching skills are needed? How might students work with different forms of representation, and how should what they have learned be evaluated? Can meaningful comparisons among students be made if students do not use the same forms of representation to display what they have learned? And should different forms of representation be combined? If so, how? Do the mental skills developed through practice using some forms of representation transfer to tasks requiring the use of other forms? The agenda, as you can see, is formidable, and although questions of the kind I have just posed are not likely to be definitively answered—I know of few questions in the social sciences or education that are definitively answered—there are leads that we can follow and possibilities that we can pursue to get on with our work.

From Conceptualization to Curriculum

Our task, therefore, is to move from a state of conceptualization, which is what Chapters 2 and 3 were intended to do, into an exploration of what those ideas might look like in the context of curriculum development and in teaching. This will require us to be ready to reconceptualize the ways in which both curriculum and teaching are conceived. Perhaps it will be useful, by means of an example, to explore the ways in which different forms of representation might be used to help students grasp an important concept in biology. Let us examine the concept "metamorphosis."

The word itself without a referent is nothing more than a noise. It becomes meaningful as students have a form of experience with living things undergoing a particular process of change and associate that experience with the word and the contexts in which it appears. Our pedagogical task is to help students understand the meaning of the term in the context of biology and, perhaps, to recognize that it has nonbiological counterparts in other areas of life. One straightforward (and probably ineffective) way this can be done is for a teacher simply to use the word and to tell a group of students what it means. It is likely that in this process a teacher would use examples designed to enable students to imagine—that is, to visualize—the process that the teacher hopes they will understand. A teacher could also show students the process through a video or film. Through fast frame cinematography of a caterpillar spinning a cocoon and changing into a butterfly, students can notice the ways in which biological transformation occurs and, through a type of observation made possible through technology, grasp the meaning of the term.

The teacher need not stop with visual examples related to biology. The concept "metamorphosis" can also be related to other aspects of life. Musical passages can be transformed in ways that are analogous to the transformation of the caterpillar into a butterfly. Analogies of the process of metamorphosis can be employed as villages become towns, and towns become cities. Where else is metamorphosis to be found? Can it be found in dance? In poetry? Can students be helped to grasp the concept in the various forms in which it lives? And what will the use and variety of such examples mean for students who are better able to deal with visual, auditory, or dynamic forms than with words alone?

There is an argument to be made that the biological conception of metamorphosis is specific to the discipline and that unless *that* particular meaning is secured, no biology has been learned. To use a tautology, to know the biological meaning of metamorphosis is to know its biological meaning.

At one level, this argument is unassailable, yet as a means of fostering understanding it is pedagogically limited: teachers have historically used analogies and examples. The point of an example is that it exemplifies; the students' task is not to take the example for the whole but, rather, to use it to grasp the meaning of the whole. Reliance on linguistic examples alone may very well limit what some students are able to understand. Furthermore, there are certain cognitive utilities in developing an individual's ability to work with analogies; recognizing the metaphorically rendered metamorphosis of villages to towns to cities might be a useful way to understand both cities and biology. Indeed, Arthur Koestler (1949) relates the process of creativity to what he calls "bisociation," a process in which two conceptual fields that were psychologically distinct are given a fresh and novel productive relationship. The cultivation of such cognitive processes might be fostered through in the kinds of examples I have just provided.

Before they are acculturated to right-angled modes of thought, young children frequently employ such thinking. When my son was three or four years of age, he asked me after I had returned home from a trip what kind of airplane I had taken. Not being an astute observer of airplane types, I told him I was on a jet plane, but I did not know what kind of jet it was. He then asked me, "Was it like George Washington?" I was puzzled. He then put his two small fists to the sides of his head and asked, "Was it like George Washington?" I grasped what he meant. Did it have "curls" (jets) on the sides of its tail section? I told him it did not; it had jets on its wings.

My son did not have a name for the type of plane I was flying—nor did I. But he did have a visual concept of it, and he was able to use a visual analogue, a portrait of George Washington, curls and all, to help me provide him with an answer to satisfy his curiosity. To do this, he had to creatively find an analogue between the look of a particular jet aircraft and the look of something else. He found it on the face of a one-dollar bill.

It seems to me that the kind of processing that my son and other preschoolers engage in is precisely the kind of thinking we ought to keep alive in schools. This can be done as long as we recognize the value of what young children do and provide opportunities for those processes to be practiced and refined. The use of multiple forms of representation by both teachers and students to exemplify and convey meaning is one way this can be achieved.

Consider another example. Historical timelines are commonly used to transform temporal conditions into visual ones. There is, of course, no literal isomorphism between time and space, yet we can imagine such relationships as we think about distances that are relative to each other. Somehow we have the capacity to assume a common velocity across space, thus making it possible to illustrate time through distance. The timeline illustrates through spacial abstraction the temporal relationships we would like our students to grasp.

There are many devices that humans have created to represent and to study the world in which we live. Maps present to us landmasses that we cannot see; histograms, scattergrams, and pie charts make visible quantitative relationships that would be obscured by number. Abacuses help keep track of numerical relationships, clocks record time, and the song lines of aboriginal peoples give spiritual significance to their environment. Models in science present synchronically numerical patterns that would otherwise be extremely difficult to comprehend diachronically. And now, through computers, those relationships can, in addition, be manipulated. Holographers are now able to use holography to make observations that would have been impossible before its invention, like the manipulation of relationships in the third dimension. In sum, these devices perform important epistemic functions not only by facilitating the display and acquisition of information but by facilitating inquiry into the information provided.

Forms of representation can not only contribute to a deeper understanding of a field of study as it is conventionally defined; they can also help redefine what is typically thought to define the nature of the field itself. Consider history.

Is history the text that historians write about the past? Or is history the past about which historians write? Normally, when we think about history, we think about books in which historians reveal their interpretation of the events of the past: Thucydides' *History of the Pelopennesian War*, Gibbon's *Decline and Fall of the Roman Empire* (1788/1963), McNeill's *The Rise of the West* (1963), Toynbee's *The World and the West* (1953), and the like. We think of Tuchman's *The Guns of August* (1962) or Shirer's *Rise and Fall of the Third Reich* (1960). History is a category in our libraries and a subject in our schools in which the historical text is central. History is narrative.

Yet history can also be conceived of as the events themselves, the culture, and the people about which historians write. This view of history makes text only one of several possible sources for historical understanding. If history is the past, then the construction of historical understanding need not be restricted to text alone. Music, art, poetry, dance, architecture, the rites and rituals of a people, the folksay, the food—in short, *any* resource, any form of representation that sheds light on the past is relevant to historical understanding. This understanding need not be couched in language.

The educational import of this view of history is significant on a number of counts. First, it expands the channels through which students have the opportunity to learn; not all students need to pass through the eye of a written text. Pictures are also relevant. So is music. Second, the meanings such forms are able to yield to the competent viewer or listener are not identical with those available to the reader of text. Architecture, for example, can disclose what text cannot say—architecture and text simply occupy two different though interacting realms of human experience. Conversely, text can convey what architecture cannot display. Thus, our understanding of the past is not only a function of the meanings that are construable from the forms themselves; it also depends upon our ability to "read" those forms. Third, this view of the concept "history" shifts from one belonging solely to the narratives written by historians to meanings about the past derived from whatever forms provide insight into its features. With this view, resources for the teaching of history expand: Curriculum planners and others concerned with the formulation of curricular activities and curricular materials can enlarge the conceptual universes through which historical understanding can be fostered. What was once the province of the textbook now includes nontext forms and in so doing enlarges the likelihood that historical understanding will be increased not only for those for whom text is not the most felicitous vehicle but for others as well.

To illustrate the differences in the information provided by text and by image, I ask you to participate in a small experiment. On the last page of this chapter is a photograph that I am going to describe in considerable detail. I do not want you to look at the picture (and I hope you have not peeked thus far). I would like you to imagine what the picture looks like on the basis of my written description. Then, when you have finished reading my description, I would like you to look at the picture and to compare the information that you received from the picture with the image you constructed from my text. What I want you to note is both discrepancy and overlap between the image you imagined and the picture you saw.

> The picture I am describing is a black-and-white photograph four and one-half inches by seven inches in dimension. The image reads horizontally, rather than vertically. It shows two people, a man about fifty-five years old sitting next to a woman of about the same age. They sit at a counter in a restaurant. He holds a small piece of bread in his left hand, his elbows on the counter. She leans toward him; her left hand rests on the edge of his shoulder and her right hand on the counter. He has a moustache and wears an open-collar shirt with a white T-shirt underneath. His shirt sleeves are rolled about halfway up his forearms. He also wears suspenders, which are about an inch wide. She wears a print shirt displaying large white daisies on a medium-dark background. Over her shirt is a dark vest.
>
> The man's hair is brushed back; his hairline is receding. She wears glasses; her hair is dark, subtly streaked with grey.
>
> Perhaps one of the most striking features of the image is that her head is about five inches from his and her expression, as she leans toward him, displays either a pucker as if she is about to kiss him or a whisper as if she is about to tell him something she wants him alone to hear. He looks directly into her eyes. This, on its face, is not a romantic scene, but one expressing camaraderie; these two seem as though they are friends.
>
> On the counter before them is a glass of milk, about a quarter

of which has been drunk, a black plastic ashtray, a large salt shaker, and a napkin holder. Each has a plate before them—her's empty, his nearly so.

They sit in a café that has a television set in the background. The overall character of the room says "not expensive." On the wall of the café, on the right side of the photograph, is the head of a stuffed deer. Over the man's head on the wall behind him is the stuffed head of a goat. No other people can be seen in the room.

Now try to create a consolidated image that my description has made possible. Reflect on that image, then turn to the photo at the end of the chapter. Compare the photo to the image you constructed. What does your image look like compared to the photo? What information do you receive from the photo that you did not receive from the descriptive text? Is there a way of using text to replicate the photo? If so, what would the text have to say? If not, what implications does the incompleteness of text have for understanding the world through text?

I suspect that the character of each of the people I have tried to describe, the particular stretch of the woman as she leans towards him, the man's particular countenance, and the expression with which he greets her words (or kiss?) are not fully describable through text, even for the most skilled writer; but once a skilled writer sees such a scene, he or she can help others through text try to see what he or she has seen. For example, the photograph I have described not only displays the features I have called to your attention, it also displays a visual composition that is triangular in form; the counter-top provides a base and the arms and angles of the man's and woman's side lead to an invisible apex near the top of the photograph. Text can call such features to the viewer's attention. And, of course, what is relevant to call to someone's attention depends on the task at hand. Ethnographers may be far more interested in the man's suspenders, his moustache, her blouse. An artist might be much more interested in the triangular composition I have just described. In each case, text can provide pointers, cues to expand awareness of the qualities to which the text refers. Text, however, even the most precise and powerful, will leave out those visual qualities the writer cannot render. The greater the particularity of the visual qualities, the more challenging is the writer's task.

Consider another example. This one is found in Figure 4.1. The image comes from an advertisement that appeared in a British news-

When you're old you can become cold without even noticing it. Often without so much as a shiver.

You simply slow down.

Soon you can't be bothered to make yourself a proper meal. A slice of toast will do. And why build up the fire? You feel all right. You don't notice your body getting colder.

And you slow down.

The next thing you don't notice is your mind slowing down. Did you order the coal? You can't remember. Never mind.

Now you've really slowed down.

You feel drowsy. Even the effort of going to bed seems too much. You just nod off in the chair.

It doesn't seem to

m a t t e r   a n y   m o r

FIGURE 4.1. Use of a Combined Propositional and Visual Form of Representation

paper (Health Education Council, 1980). What we find here is a brilliant use of language and image. The gradually increasing use of space between sentences, words, and letters slows the pace of the reading, thus reinforcing the message expressed in the prose. The gradual use of increased space is something the reader does not notice until the end of the narrative. Like the elderly poor who, without heat or proper diet, succumb to the winter's cold and gradually die, readers, too, find themselves unaware that their pace is slowing, and even they eventually come to the end of the article by hanging onto an uncompleted word. Completion is prematurely terminated.

The foregoing examples were intended to illustrate the ways in which meanings are encoded within different forms of representation. The meaning you are able to construe from each is influenced by its distinctive features. The photograph yields meaning through image; the ad, through the interaction of text and image. Forms of representation abound. Cartoons, diagrams, gestures, rites and rituals, architecture, holograms, and, rapidly emerging on the horizon, multimedia—all provide means through which the contents of the human imagination can be given a public presence. Indeed, one of the unsung contributions of what might be loosely called "technology" is its capacity to invite humans to consider possibilities for the representation of their ideas that could not have taken form before the existence of the technology itself. The availability, for example, of neon tubing made it possible for sculptors to conceive of images that Michelangelo himself could not have dreamed of. It does seem probable that the flexibility and growing possibilities of computer technology, CD-ROM, and holography, for example, may lead to the birth of information displays and forms of meaning that the world has never before known. The invention of new tools makes new forms of construction possible. The building site for some of the most important is upon the fertile ground of the human imagination.

Will those of us responsible for the conduct of educational practice and the policies that affect it exploit these newfound potentialities? It seems clear that the presence of these technologies within the culture does not ensure their use within the school. The most difficult task for educators may very well be relinquishing the yellow school bus mentality that conceives of both the purposes and the forms of schooling in terms conditioned by familiar and comfortable traditions. We may need to reconstruct our past, that is, to recognize its limiting assumptions and priorities, in order to invent an educational future for our children that has the capacity to invite them into the new worlds that these new technologies have made possible.

Taking such a tack leads to some important difficulties that need to be acknowledged and addressed, not the least of which are the attitudes and expectations of students regarding just what constitutes a legitimate source of knowledge. Students have virtually been conditioned to assign to text dominion—indeed sole dominion—in the province of knowledge. For many students, to know or understand means knowing what the textbook says. Their conception of knowledge is literal.

Given the emphasis that schools place on the written word, this is not surprising. Yet language as written, and especially literal language, does not exhaust by any means the sources of human understanding. Forms such as visual art, dance, music, poetry, architecture, and rituals also contribute their share. Because these forms do not have the specificity and singularity of the literal, they make different interpretations possible. Indeed, they invite them. As Singer-Gabella (1992) has pointed out, those very qualities that appear to problematize their use from one perspective also constitute their strength from another. Writing about her research on the teaching of history, she says:

> The quest to provide students an alternative vision of history might, I would conjecture, also be assisted by the very forms of representation I have argued are so problematic. In historical inquiry, the equivalent of generating complex algorithms is generating interpretations: probing events, naming their significance, and relating them to a larger web of historical understanding. During interviews, I found that if students more readily pointed to the textbook as the repository of historical facts, they seemed more able to generate interpretations about painting, photography, poetry, and music. Two explanations are especially plausible.
>
> The first reason lies in students' abilities to construe the human purposes, biases, and assumptions shaping music, poetry, and painting. Because students do sense human intervention in painting, music, and poetry, a contribution of these forms may be in their role as a starting point for critical analysis. Through them, students can begin to recognize the intentionality and contextual influence of human representation, and with questioning of the type Lampert models, identify the human voice even in seemingly more objective representational forms like the textbook or photography. Hence, the integration of diverse forms of representation into the history curriculum may be essential both because they provide different visions, *and* because students more readily see them as voices to be challenged; more readily enter into dialogue with their human creators. In drawing on non-discursive forms, we may both enable students to partake in the inquiry, and also challenge their epistemologies. (pp. 19–20)

Singer-Gabella goes on to remind us that Susanne Langer (1957) points out an important difference between the discursive forms used in propositional language and those nondiscursive forms used in the arts. The latter are especially appropriate, in Langer's view, for representing the life of feeling. Discursive representation employs a conventionalized relationship between a symbol and its referent. In addition, through the conventional uses of syntax, the terms employed in discursive propositions can be combined not only to create new meanings but to alter them without the loss of meaning. For example, the word *niece* can be defined as "one's sibling's daughter." In non-discursive forms, the substitution of one quality—say a color, or a sound, or a poetic term for another—has no equivalence. In nondiscursive forms, when you change a part, you change the whole in which it participates.

When students believe the text possesses a single correct meaning, it is not difficult to understand why they would regard their task as discovering the correct one, storing it in their memory bank, and being ready to retrieve it when called upon to do so. Being smart means being right, and being right means knowing the single correct literal answer to questions that might be posed.

Such an attitude toward understanding does little to promote intellectual values that celebrate multiple perspectives, judgment, risk taking, speculation, and interpretation. Visual images, music, dance, and other nonliteral forms can invite modes of thinking that reflect the foregoing values. When everything is clearly specified, the need to interpret is diminished; the problem for the student is to converge upon Truth.[1] The meaning of a Gothic cathedral as symptomatic of the beliefs and values of the Middle Ages in France or England is determined through interpretation and speculation. Yet, as Singer-Gabella points out elsewhere in her paper, students are prone to disregard architecture as a "real" source of historical understanding. Unfortunately, through the use of multiple-choice tests and limiting forms of teaching, our schools have succeeded in promoting a narrow, fact-oriented conception of what it means to know. This conception assigns a privileged place to propositional discourse.

Ambiguity, then, if that is the right term, has its cognitive virtues. A school culture that fosters the quest for certainty encourages dispositions antithetical to the intellectual life. Intellectual life is characterized by the absence of certainty, by the inclination to see things from more than one angle, by the thrill of the search more than the closure of the find. Forms of representation that encourage such dispositions are closer to the heart of that life than those that lead students away from it.

I cannot help but comment that many of the qualities I have described as being close to the heart of intellectual life are often found in profusion in educational settings often regarded as anything but intellectual. I speak in particular of the well-run kindergarten. It is in the well-run kindergarten that all of the children's senses are engaged with a rich array of sensory material that they are encouraged to explore. It is in the kindergarten that engagement in the process of exploration without a specific objective in mind is common currency. It is in the kindergarten that purposes evolve in the process of engagement. And it is in the kindergarten where the child's personal interpretation is prized.

Come first grade, in many classrooms, schools become "serious."[2] "Serious" means mastering social conventions; learning your letters and how to make them properly; learning how to read, add, and subtract; and the like. The sensory-rich environment of the kindergarten is, in too many primary grade classrooms, reduced to a heavy, right-angled emphasis on the three Rs and on literal meaning. In the process of academic socialization the spirit of exploration and imagination characteristic of kindergarten gets converted through a literal-orientated environment focused on academic achievement. This shift in spirit, for the most part, remains a dominant feature of schooling through graduate school.

One other point regarding kindergarten and the "seriousness" of the primary grades. I have made the point that the presence of a wide array of forms of representation is characteristic of the kindergarten and that as children proceed into the first grade and beyond, there is a systematic diminution of the use of these forms. I have also indicated that the major mission of the primary grades is to enable children to acquire and learn to use the conventions we call the three Rs. The emphasis is on what Jackson (1986) calls "mimetic teaching." Mimetic teaching places a premium on the transmission of culture. Its aim is to get children to acquire known skills or bodies of knowledge, to pass on, as it were, the codes and skills of the culture. The child's task, in a sense, is to "absorb" this content; the learning is replicative (Broudy, Smith, & Burnett, 1964).

In kindergarten, mimetic teaching is nowhere near as central. In kindergarten, expressivity and discovery are important. Imagination matters. Personal exploration counts. In short, the tenor of the kindergarten differs from the tenor of the primary grades. What matters is not only that multiple forms of representation be available, but that there is a climate of expectation that supports their exploration outside of the boundaries of "right answers." Put another way, both the presence of different forms of representation and a context that encourages their imaginative use are important features of educationally effective settings.

Implementing Curricula

We return to the task before us: the transformation of the ideas in Chapters 2 and 3 into an array of resources and pedagogical practices that can be used to expand and deepen students' understanding of a field of study. A review of the research literature in the social studies, a field where one might expect the integration of diverse forms of representation to be most prevalent, reveals little empirical research available to assess the effects of integrated curricula on what students understand in the field. What is available are two doctoral dissertations, one done at Harvard University by Terrie Epstein (1989) and the other, a small part of which we have already encountered, done at Stanford University by Marcy Singer (1991).

Epstein's (1989) study investigated the practical application of the idea of multiple forms of literacy elaborated in Chapters 2 and 3 to a unit in the social studies. In her study, Epstein designed a two-week social studies curriculum to help high school sophomores and juniors learn about the slavery period in America. Television programs, stories, myths, music, visual art, poetry, and other artistic forms were used to try to make the period come to life. Students watched the television production of *Roots*, they looked at pictures, they heard music, they learned about folk tales and myths; in short, the curriculum was designed to help students get into the skins of the slaves.

The processes and effects of the curriculum were evaluated through a variety of methods, including the uses of educational criticism (Eisner, 1991b) for the teaching process. Educational criticisms were prepared both by the teacher and by an independent educational critic. In addition, students' written work—the essays they wrote about their experience—and the music that some of them composed at the end of the unit to represent what they had learned were analyzed. The students also completed a questionnaire about their experiences in this curriculum. The evaluation was, therefore, a multimodal effort to secure a wide variety of different levels of information that would allow the researcher to draw credible conclusions about the effects of the approach. The results of the program were promising. Epstein wrote:

> Overall, students felt they learned from and liked the materials and methods represented in class and found the approach an improvement over more common social studies practices. Throughout the

interviews and questionnaires, students continuously commented
that the curriculum gave them a feel or picture of what slavery was
really like. As a result, they learned more from it than from a
textbook, which they perceived either as an assemblage of facts,
one person's views, or an account removed from the reality of the
experience.

Most students also enjoyed and learned from the project. They
liked not having to memorize facts and appreciated having a choice
in evaluation and an opportunity to express their own ideas and
feelings. Most felt they would have done a better job if they had
spent more time on the project, and if the teacher had given better
direction or more class time.

Five students felt the essay test was a fairer measure of their
learning. Some of these students might have benefitted from more
direction and a project. Others simply may feel more comfortable
expressing their thoughts in essay form under any circumstances.
(pp. 209–210)

Although Epstein's results could be due to the Hawthorne effect,
the excerpts of student work included in the study and the observations made by the educational critic lend credence to the value of
using multiple forms of representation in teaching about complex
events. Epstein's study provided a beginning in the systematic inves-
tigation of the uses of the arts and other forms for enriching the
experiences of students in social studies and in broadening the array
of means students might use to represent what they have learned
from such experiences.

An example of the uses of poetry, the visual arts, and literary
narrative as means for teaching and assessing what students have
learned in the study of history is found in Epstein's (in press) research. Working with twenty self-selected eleventh-grade college-
bound high school students enrolled in a course on United States
history, Epstein and the teacher with whom she collaborated intro-
duced a unit on late nineteenth-century European and Asian immi-
gration to the United States. Students read oral histories of the immigrants, viewed nineteenth-century photographs, and interpreted
poems and cartoons about them. These sources, in addition to text,
were intended to help students secure a wide understanding of the
immigrant experience.

Students were asked to focus on two questions: First, how did
immigrants interpret their experience as immigrants? And, second,
how did reformers and nativists portray the immigrants and the immigrant experience? Working with the regular classroom teacher, Ep-

stein asked students, after they had worked with the primary sources for seven days, to represent some aspect of their understanding of the immigrant experience through an artistically grounded work that would be appraised by the representativeness and complexity of its historical themes or concepts, by the technical skill or craftsmanship it displayed, and by the "expressiveness" of the work, as judged by a reader or viewer. One example, a work that was created by a student named Hannah, displays, I think, quite vividly the kind of empathic understanding that Hannah must have had and was able to help her reader secure through the poem that she created. The following is Hannah's poem and Epstein's comments about both the poem and the teacher's interaction with Hannah about Hannah's intent and motivation in writing it.

WELCOME, TO THE PROMISED LAND

Countless
flooding faces—
some with dominating European features
others with flat Asian canvases,
they come,
merge,
and melt
into America.

Leaving watery eyes, friends
and close family members behind,
in the comfort of their world;
to experience humiliation
hatred
and unparalleled fear
in what was supposed to be
their chance,
Welcome,
to the promise.

The golden gates of
the budding, flowery flag nation.
The welcoming Ms. America
waving her eternal flame
across the harbor—
the dream.
The crowded tenement buildings
the degrading inspection of people
the foreign flesh

sold and bought, in the underground world,
the reality.

An unwanting nation
returns to Sicily and Ireland
faces stamped rejection,
bodies marred—not good enough
to have a chance.
Desolate persons
stripped of their dignity
and robbed of their dreams
of a life they expected to find,
in America.
Welcome, to the promised land
my friends,
Welcome.

Epstein comments as follows:

Hannah used poetry to portray a vivid yet subtle view of the immigrant experience from the perspectives of the immigrant and the nativist. She fits the historical knowledge she has constructed into chronological form, beginning the first verse with the nativist perception of a differentiated horde and moving in the second verse to the immigrant reminiscence of worlds and lives left behind. The chronicle continues with the juxtaposition of conflicting images of the promised land, first as a place which beckons and then as a place which betrays. The chronicle ends by depicting deportation as the loss of immigrant hope and dignity and the fulfillment of nativist promise and policy.

Hannah also uses poetic form to construct images and feelings relevant to the historical times she depicts. Alliteration is used throughout, serving to emphasize mood and make sights and sounds more memorable. Symbols evoke images of traditional American ideals, as well as immigrants' hopes and nativists' fears. Word, phrase, and verse cohere in ways which enable an engaged reader to construct images of immigrants and landscapes, feelings of fear and resentment, senses of hopes and dreams anticipated and then abandoned. Hannah has written a poem which enables the engaged reader to enter into Hannah's conception of the immigrant experience and to come away with insights into and empathy for the historical experiences represented.

When asked what she was attempting to portray in writing the poem, Hannah expressed her own empathic understanding:

HANNAH: I wanted to show the fact that they had to leave their home, leave everything they had, because they thought they had this big chance in America. They thought it was this great country and once they got there a lot of time they had bad experiences and some of them had to go home or some of them had to stay and have a bad life. So I was trying to show that—they were thinking, "Okay, we're going to leave everything we have behind and go to this great big chance" and when they got there they were made fun of and they couldn't find jobs and some of them had to go back home. So I wanted to show the hardship of that . . . that aspect of it.

TEACHER: What tone were you trying to get across?

HANNAH: Not sarcastic but in the end I was saying "welcome," sort of taking the immigrants' side, saying, "This is what you think you can have, but actually you can't have any of it." It came out a little bit more sarcastic than I intended, but the tone I was basically trying to convey was "I feel bad for them. Look what they had to go through—the hardship." It's supposed to be "that's how we feel."

TEACHER: Are you satisfied with this?

HANNAH: I thought it showed what I was trying to get across. That people are leaving something really important to them and once they get there, there's nothing or there's hardship. So I thought it portrayed that—the way I wanted it to come out.

Again, the task is one of transformation. How can we use visual, auditory, gustatory, and other forms to represent aspects of the world we hope students will come to understand? What is it that photography, video, and other visual forms can do to help students understand, say, the life processes of growing things? What does drawing reveal that the naked eye fails to see? How can slow-motion cinematography make vivid what would otherwise remain obscure? Do students learn something about the changes in a growing flower by creating a dance that portrays its development? If so, what are the characteristics of that understanding, and how is it related to the forms of representation they employed or perceived?

To illustrate the distinctive ways in which different forms of representation might portray a common experience, reflect upon the following story.

You're driving through the countryside on a quiet, uninhabited two-lane road that runs adjacent to a large green field in which there are several beautiful horses grazing. The day is bright, the sky is blue, punctuated only by large white cumulus clouds overhead. You decide to pull the car over to the side of the road adjacent to a fence to pause for awhile in order to observe the horses grazing on the grassy field beyond the fence.

As you stand by the fence, a horse far in the distance and light brown in color begins to move away from you. As the horse moves, its speed increases. From a walk to a trot, from a trot to a gallop, from a gallop to a full run. As its speed increases, the color of the horse changes slowly from a light brown to a deep purple. In addition, wings, white in color, grow out of its back. As the horse runs across the field, its large white wings begin to move up and down, up and down, and it starts to rise into the light blue sky, its size diminishing with each second past; and finally, it penetrates a large white cumulus cloud and disappears from sight.

Imagine yourself being asked to represent your experience to others. What might you do if asked to write a poem about your experience, to perform a dance, to tell a story, to give a literal account, to paint a picture, or to sculpt an image of the event? Each of these forms would, no doubt, impose their own constraints and provide their own opportunities. Each would place particular demands upon your skills. For some forms of representation, you might be well equipped; others would be little more than sources of frustration. The forms you know how to use would give you opportunities for representation unavailable to you in those forms for which you lack the necessary skills. Furthermore, even with highly refined skills, what you are able to represent would be influenced by the representational possibilities of the forms you were asked to use. If you could combine forms of representation, new possibilities would emerge. In sum, what you are able to convey would depend upon the skills you possessed relative to the forms you are able to use, the potentialities of the forms themselves, and, of course, the extent to which your imaginative life made visions of those potentialities options you could consider.

It is of more than passing interest to note that in much of our social life we have the option of selecting the form or forms of representation we choose to portray our experience. Given a trip to Venice, for example, some people write about it, others take photos, others paint, still others tell stories or use other forms of high drama. It is this diversity of representation that contributes to the commonweal by making public our own experience in ways and through forms that we uniquely invest with meaning. Indeed, we learn most from those whose contributions we could not have created ourselves.

Consider the account of one teacher as he recalls his efforts to help students see relationships between subjects and notice how he uses different forms of representation in this process.

> Science and art are considered opposites in school and by thinking it teachers make it so. Recently the opposite of this happened with a group of students I was working with. We started out by telling a collective story—one line each. As the story evolved the main characters would find themselves in difficult positions and would escape by transforming themselves into animals. I followed the theme of transformation by suggesting that we all transform ourselves into anything we wanted, and write a description from the point of view of the creature we became. The students became cats, flies, caterpillars, in one case a boiling potato, and in another a withering Aztec god. I became a left hand.
>
> After writing we drew pictures of the world through the eyes of our creature selves and then did an improvisation. We became physically the creatures we were transformed into. We then had to create some relationship with each other. One of the girls in considering that problem in improvisation asked me if a boiling potato could worship a withering Aztec god.
>
> From the transformation of ourselves we began to talk about magical transformation, and about the transformation of physical objects. This naturally led to alchemy and from there to chemistry. This whole experience led me to understand chemistry in a new and exciting way and to restore some of the magic of chemical change that had been lost for me in school through tediously having to memorize formulas and facts. (Kohl, 1969, pp. 65–66)

The ability to use one or more forms of representation is not only a function of opportunities for students to acquire the necessary skills; it is also related to the aptitudes or proclivities that they possess. For some students, language is the most powerful means they can use to represent their experience. Others find visual images, say painting or photography, much more congenial. Their aptitudes interact with opportunities to learn. Thus, when a school defines its curricular agenda, it also defines the opportunities students will have to encounter forms of representation related to their aptitudes or interests. The features of this agenda are critical for several reasons. First, the availability of different forms of representation contribute significantly to educational equity. When schools limit forms of representation to number and word, children whose aptitudes are in areas other than word and number are handicapped. Such children have fewer opportunities to find a place in our educational sun. Second, the kind of diversity that schools, I believe, should cultivate is diminished when a single-minded emphasis on a rather narrow range of forms prevails. The absence of opportunity reduces the chances for cultivating productive idiosyncrasy. Third, unfair status advantages are conferred upon students whose aptitudes are congruent with the forms employed. Indeed, it will be difficult to equalize status among children without a corresponding equalization in the ways in which society at large, universities, and the schools themselves regard the relative value of different human abilities.

One important effort to help teachers learn how to help students appreciate differences in aptitude relative to different task demands is Elizabeth Cohen's (1986) work in complex instruction. Cohen makes the point that status equalization among students is facilitated by the use of curricular group tasks that call for different kinds of intellectual skills. By providing such tasks in the classroom and by helping children who engage in them recognize the need for different skills and the fact that different children in the group possess them, greater status equalization is likely. Both the task *and* the recognition of the need for different skills or aptitudes are necessary. Cohen finds that when such tasks are provided and when teachers help students realize that different abilities are needed for solving complex problems, levels of participation among previously marginalized or low-participating students are increased. The use of such methods, Cohen believes, is important for all children, but especially so for those coming from minority groups, since they are more likely to be marginalized in schools than their majority counterparts.

There is no question that complex tasks—by definition—require different sorts of skills, skills that often relate to different forms of representation and that require different kinds of problem-solving abilities. When such tasks are made available—and this is a curriculum development problem as well as a pedagogical problem—opportunities for students to achieve competence and recognition are increased, *provided* the school values such accomplishment. However, that schools equally value different cognitive skills should not be taken for granted. The devaluation of some forms of cognition is especially acute at the university level.

At the risk of belaboring the point, I cannot refrain from commenting on the conservative influence of universities on the aims, content, and form of secondary education, indeed even on middle and primary schools.

Parents are understandably interested in the academic success of their children. They recognize that admission to universities, particularly selective universities, will require high levels of skill in language and mathematics; the SATs operationalize such skills. Parents also understand that certain courses are "more equal" than others. University admissions committees establish policies that publicly define, for many high school students, the courses they are expected to take (Stanford University, 1990). These courses are often referred to as solids (something substantial) as contrasted with liquids or gases (courses with little or no substance). As a result of these expectations and the printed messages received from the universities, a limited and stereotypical conception of human ability is fostered, high school programs are constructed that reflect the stereotypes on which they are based, and certain students are effectively dissuaded from courses in which they have a deep and genuine interest and in which they might do very well. Ironically, all of this is justified in the name of rigor, standards, and intellect. In reality, the underlying assumptions represent a parochial view of both human ability and the possibilities of education. In the long run, this view, reflected in educational policy, depletes the resources that the society as a whole might receive had students' aptitudes been cultivated. Taking courses in the arts in secondary schools, for example, is risky business for students wishing access to Harvard, Chicago, or Stanford. In addition, there is no room on the SATs for students to display their aptitudes or interests in these and related areas.[3]

There is a lesson to be learned from the foregoing: the content and standards of important educational rites of passage and the impact of high-stake tests must be central considerations in any effort to reform, restructure, or reculture schools. Trying to promote curricular diversity or multiple forms of intelligence (Gardner, 1983), trying to provide opportunities for the realization of different aptitudes or the cultivation of particular talents will continue to be difficult without a widening of the gates through which students must pass if they are to reach the "highest" levels of educational attainment. To bring about such changes will require teachers and school administrators (and professors of education) to work much more closely than we have with universities and their admissions committees.[4]

Thus far, I have emphasized the importance of building school programs that make it possible for students to encounter and use diverse forms of representation. My major aim has been to underscore the idea that humans represent the world through a wide variety of forms and that each of these forms, either singly or in combination with others, makes particular kinds of meaning possible. I have also emphasized the importance of making educational equity real for children of different aptitudes by giving them access to forms in which their aptitudes might be used. The restriction of educational opportunity is no less significant within the curriculum itself than in denying children access to the school. What is important for children is not only having access to a school, but also finding programs that are congenial to their aptitudes or forms of intelligence when they arrive. The availability of diverse forms of representation provides such access.

Making Learning Problem-Centered

Yet the availability of diverse forms is insufficient. What one does with such forms must also be taken into account. Here I wish to emphasize what Dewey himself emphasized in his own curricular thinking. I speak of the importance of problem-centered learning, a phrase that has gained recent saliency, although its roots certainly are located in the best of progressive educational theory (Kilpatrick, 1919).

Problem-centered tasks are tasks in which there is a problem to solve, one about which students care and which often, but not necessarily always, they will have had a hand in formulating. By engaging students in the conceptualization of a problem, they are invited to exercise the best of their analytic and speculative abilities. When the problem is one that is genuinely meaningful to them, they are much more likely to become stakeholders in the problem rather than people who simply execute the purposes of another—which, incidentally, was Plato's definition of a slave.

The ways in which problems are defined in school by students often reflect what they believe to be an acceptable form of intellectual or academic work. Thus, inviting students to think about the ways in which visual forms might be used to portray an array of mathematical relationships, a period in history, a set of ideas in one of the natural sciences, and the like is also an invitation for them to think *within* the form itself (Dewey, 1934/1958). Children, in effect, become smarter as their experience (and skill) in coping with such demands increases. Architects, for example, become extremely flexible and fluent in the

kinds of solutions they can generate to any single set of spacial problems. Put succinctly, the best way I know of to develop metaphorical
forms of thinking is to have many opportunities to think metaphorically. The best way I know of to think musically is to have many
opportunities to engage in musical cognition. The best way I know of
to learn how to use your body in relation to music is to have many
opportunities to learn how to dance. These "truisms" seem patently
obvious except, it seems, to those who make educational policy and
plan school programs. As I indicated earlier, kindergarten is one of
the few places in the school that takes such considerations into account in a serious and sustained way. Our own rather parochial conception of intellect and narrow view of the skills children need typically lead to a rather meager educational agenda. It is an agenda that,
in effect, limits what children can learn and that leaves fallow the
fields in which their aptitudes might be cultivated.

There is one institution I know that does pay a serious attention
to the use of multiple aptitudes and the development of diverse forms
of knowing. I speak of Waldorf schools. Founded in 1919 by Rudolf
Steiner, Waldorf schools have been established throughout the world.
At present, there are over 500 schools in 37 countries (Uhrmacher,
1991). Waldorf education is based upon a view of human development that acknowledges the importance of the sensory system and
the role of the body in learning. It attaches a special significance to
the importance of myth and folk tale, and to eurythmy, a form of
bodily movement designed to harmonize the various aspects of the
child's experience. It emphasizes the importance of image making in
children's learning. Its teachers utilize rhythm and other sensory
forms to help students understand ideas in arithmetic. In short,
Waldorf schools, unlike most American public schools, provide, or
attempt to provide, a program that affords children a balanced educational diet, one that not only fosters conventional forms of academic
achievement but also puts a premium on the development of imagination and the refinement of the sensibilities.

It is significant, I think, that curriculum planners are increasingly
advocating a less compartmentalized and more integrated approach
to curriculum. During the heyday of the curriculum reform movement in the 1960's, the structure of the disciplines was *the* flagship
idea guiding the direction of curriculum thinking (Bruner, 1961). In
this approach to curriculum reform, each discipline—mathematics,
biology, chemistry, physics—was thought to have its own unique
conceptual structure. To understand a discipline, students needed to
understand its structure. Since disciplinary structures are considered

unique, it meant, for all practical purposes, that each discipline needed to be taught as an independent entity. Integration among disciplines was not encouraged; indeed, integration was thought to complicate the students' comprehension of the discipline.

One of the developments that has occurred in the field of curriculum since the 1960's is the recognition that school programs need to be made more meaningful for students, that getting students to think like biologists, as the slogan went, might not be the most educationally relevant aspiration for the vast majority of students (Bruner, 1971). Students need to see the connection between what they study in school and the life that they lead outside school. They need to have their knowledge situated in tasks and relationships somewhat like those they will encounter outside school if the transfer of learning is to occur (Greeno, 1989). Life outside school does not come packaged in the conceptually tidy tasks that the structure of a discipline represents; hence a focus on that structure can increase the isolation of the disciplines and may, in fact, diminish rather than increase the student's ability to transfer what he or she has learned.

One of the ways to increase relevance and transfer is to help students see relationships across fields; another is to increase the variety of forms of representation through which meanings can be construed by the student. Thus, increasing the variety of forms used to teach a field and relating that field to other fields, or using a variety of fields to address a key idea, are ways not only to provide more handles for students to grasp but also to make what students learn more transferable.

This integrated orientation to curriculum planning is reflected in the history–social science curriculum framework for California public schools (1987). The California framework encourages curriculum planners to draw upon a wide array of resources to help students of all ages understand aspects of history and culture: music, poetry, stories, visual art. It tries to blur the boundaries.

There may very well be a trade-off between the tidiness of a discipline-centered approach and the potentially confusing richness of the approach reflected in the California framework. Yet I believe that the transfer problem for students is so formidable and school subject matter so bookish and insular that efforts to expand the resources from which students may learn is worth the potential difficulties those resources might present. We cannot continue to offer programs in schools in which high levels of student performance predict nothing but performance on school-situated tasks. If school performance is only useful for predicting success at more schooling, the practical meaning of what students learn in school for their life outside school will be small or nonexistent. We need to rethink the aims we seek to achieve as well as the conditions, structures, and activities we use to achieve them.

How might the kind of curriculum activities I have suggested be developed? How does one create materials and learning activities in which the senses come into play as they interact with different forms of representation? First, it seems to me that their creation requires a willingness to give up old habits and routines and to think about curriculum planning in ways that exploit the capacities I have described. How does a teacher think about physics, history, the social studies, music, and art in ways that provide children with opportunities to connect to these fields with their entire sensorium? Can one think about music visually? Can one think about visual arts musically? What about physics and biology, chemistry and mathematics? Are there activities and materials that can be employed that make such relationships possible? Answers to such questions clearly require an educational imagination, but that imagination is not likely to be used unless there is an appetite to do so. But even when that appetite is present, there will still be a need for teachers to have the time to plan and to acquire the skills necessary to create the kind of materials that usefully might accompany the activities that they have planned.

In some school districts, there are curriculum development centers in which teachers are helped by graphic artists and technicians to create instructional materials especially suited to their educational purposes. Teachers who need specific kinds of graphics for overheads can get them. Those who require noncommercial instructional devices can be helped to fabricate them. I envision a time in which there will be a center in a school or school district that helps teachers create the materials they need so that they are able to build the kinds of programs they desire.

Such a resource would give new meaning to the term *curriculum specialist*. A curriculum specialist would have the skills and the responsibility for helping teachers create the materials they need to achieve their aims. Where materials or other resources were commercially available, the curriculum specialist might be in a position to know where and how to get them.

Summing Up the Argument

The argument that I have advanced has, you might say, two parts. First, I have argued that humans have an inherent need to make meaning and that forms of representation are means through which different kinds of meaning can be made. From that perspective, education as a process concerned with fostering an individual's ability to construct, diversify, and deepen meaning should make it possible for students to become skilled in the construction of such meanings within a variety of the forms that are available.

Second, I have argued that there is an important relationship between individual aptitudes and the forms of representation individuals are likely to be able to use well. When the curriculum of the school defines representational options narrowly—when such options are largely restricted to the use of literal language and number, for example—it creates educational inequities and, moreover, fails to develop the aptitudes that many individual students possess. This in turn exacts a cost from the society at large, since the development of aptitudes is perhaps the major means through which humans contribute to the commonweal.

The foregoing ideas have relevance not only for curriculum; they have relevance for evaluation as well. For example, it is possible to afford students opportunities to represent what they have come to know about a subject of study through forms that are congruent with their aptitudes. Both Singer-Gabella and Epstein provided such opportunities in their studies. Some students might represent their understanding through visual images, others through literal language, others through choreographed movement, others through literary and poetic forms. While I do not believe that such options must always be made available, I do believe that it is important, from time to time, to give students the opportunities to represent their experience through a form of representation of their choosing. As I have already indicated, in life outside of school this is precisely what occurs. Different individuals represent their experience in different ways; and because they do, the culture at large is enriched.

Such a practice will of course increase the difficulty of making comparisons among the performances of students. But whether the comparative ranking of students is in the long-term best interests of either the students or the society is something that one can certainly argue. In the context of education, the creation of conditions that lead to self-realization is, I believe, a primary aim. If the means through which such realization can occur makes comparative assessments more difficult, so be it. Education is not a horse race. Speed is not the ultimate virtue. What people can become through an educationally caring community is. The provision of opportunities for youngsters, indeed the invitation to use means that draw upon their strengths, is a practice that can be fostered and its consequences appraised. It seems to me that such a practice has much to commend it, despite the complexities it is likely to engender.[5]

In Retrospect

How might I summarize the major ideas I have tried to develop in this slender volume? First, I have tried to make the case that the separation of the mind from the body, a separation initiated by Plato and given a strong forward thrust by Descartes, has contributed to a narrow conception of intellect. Second, I have argued that our sensory system is our first avenue to consciousness and that its development and refinement is what makes concept formation possible. Third, I have argued further that the images that we call concepts are transformed and made public through a variety of forms of representation available in the culture and that each of these forms makes it possible for individuals to both construct and experience particular kinds of meanings. These meanings are directly related to the potentialities and the constraints that each of these forms provides. Any form of representation both reveals and conceals. Fourth, I have argued that our dominant conception of knowledge—a conception, in the main, restricted to true propositions having scientific warrant—is far too limited a view of what human understanding entails.

Humans both understand and reason about the world in a variety of ways. These ways manifest themselves in the forms of representation they are able to use. Hence I believe that one major aim of education is the expansion and deepening of the meanings individuals can secure in their life, and since I believe that humans have different aptitudes with respect to the forms in which meanings can be made, I believe that school programs should provide ample opportunity for youngsters to become "literate" in a wide variety of forms. This will increase the meanings all students can secure and expand educational opportunities for those students whose aptitudes are most congruent with those forms now neglected.

At a practical level, the ideas I have developed here require a transformation of the ways in which we teach, the curriculum resources we employ, and the forms we allow students to use in order to represent what they have come to know. This practical transformation requires a reconceptualization of what we regard as intellect; as long as our sensory system is regarded as of marginal importance in human cognition and as long as schools are concerned with the development of a narrow conception of knowledge, it is not likely that the ideas I have developed in this book will find a home in our schools. We need to reconceive the ways in which we think about mind, understanding, the practice of teaching, and the aims, content, and form of curricula. These are no small matters. Furthermore, to create the kinds of resources that are needed will require both time and money. Teachers, many of whom know in their bones that children need what is euphemistically referred to as "hands-on experience" and who wish to make such experience possible, will need the time and support to acquire or to create the kind of materials and tasks that are relevant to such experience. Evaluation practices will need to be liberalized so that both students and teachers have permission to use forms that traditionally have not been real options.

A major theme of this book is the problem of how those concerned with improving schools should decide what educational aims to pursue and what content to teach. Throughout its pages, three important ideas have been discussed as relevant to this question. The first is the idea of *forms of representation,* those sensory qualities used in the culture to generate the symbolic forms we call art, music, dance, poetry, literary text, mathematics, science, and the like. I have argued that each form of representation carries with it its own parameters of possibility for the construction and recovery of meaning. One major aim of education—perhaps its most important aim—is to enable individuals to acquire the kinds of cognitive skills that will enable them to construe meanings from the forms in which they appear.

Second, I have argued that each form of representation is potentially subject to different *modes of treatment.* Language, for example, can be treated in both literal and literary ways. The literal emphasizes a conventional mode of treatment, while the literary emphasizes an expressive mode. The same is true with respect to the fine arts. Music can be treated in a mimetic fashion, or it can be treated expressively. Knowing the ways in which forms of representation can be treated means knowing the potentialities they possess for the representation of meaning. Fostering our understanding of these potentialities and having experience in their use ought to be, in my view, essential features of the programs we provide in schools.

I also indicated that each form of representation can be variably located on a *syntactical structure* that extends from the rule governed to the figurative. That is to say, some syntactical requirements demand fealty to rule-governed procedures, while others invite idiosyncratic use in ways that often violate existing norms. Students should have experience exploring how forms of representation can be used in various locations on this syntactical continuum.

The educational purposes served by such experience are several. First, the ability to encode and decode forms of representation makes possible meanings specific to the forms employed. Second, the cognitive skills that humans develop are related to the forms of thinking they have an opportunity to practice. Different forms of representation, different modes of treatment, and problems located in different areas on the syntactical continuum provide students the opportunity to practice, develop, and refine such thinking. Third, because individual students possess different aptitudes, the opportunities they encounter in school, opportunities defined by the school's curriculum, provide them with access to success or the probability of defeat. I have argued that a broad array of opportunities represented by a wide array of forms of representation and modes of treatment, as well as the uses of different syntactical procedures, increases educational equity for students by increasing the probability that they will be able to play to their strengths.

Finally, I have argued that the provision of such a program within the school has, as its ultimate beneficiary, not only the student but also the culture in which we all live. Our experience as individuals is significantly influenced by the contributions of others. As schools make it possible for students to optimize the realization of their potentialities in these matters, the culture itself is enriched. Students are not only a part of our culture; they are a part of our future and we are a part of theirs. Thus, the educational agenda that I have described is one built upon a broad conception of mind, a multiple conception of meaning, and the ambition to create genuinely educative and equitable schools. Educational equity is not likely without a range of opportunities for conception and representation, opportunities that are wide enough to satisfy the diversity of talents of those who come to school and who share their future with us.

As we seek genuinely to reform American schools we will need to release ourselves from the grips of traditional stereotypes about what schools should be, how teaching is to proceed, what appropriate curriculum content entails, and how evaluation should occur. We need to free ourselves from ideas and practices that do not serve our students well and that, in turn, generate significant inequities in children's life chances. The view of mind and knowledge that I have tried to advance in this book is intended to contribute to the reconceptualization that is necessary. Reconceptualization, although it is a necessary condition, is not sufficient. In the end, reconceptualization must lead to practical consequences. A challenging agenda remains before us.

James F. Danis, 1988

Mac and Jo, Healy Hotel, Alaska 1973 #54

Notes

Chapter 1

1. It is interesting to note that both a *Nation at Risk* and *America 2000* employ military metaphors to make their point. *A Nation at Risk* imagines the prospects to the United States due to invasion by a foreign army, and *America 2000* celebrates the achievement of Desert Storm. Why military metaphors are chosen to address school reform and the education of the young is not altogether clear, but one would have little difficulty, I think, finding metaphors more congruent with the aims of education and the development of children and adolescents.

2. A technicist orientation to any task seeks universal procedures, that is, procedures that will overcome the idiosyncrasies of individual contexts. What one wants is "the one best method." This aspiration is not unrelated to a conception of science that seeks to discover universal laws that will make it possible to control and predict the phenomenon being addressed. Efficiency and effectiveness are regarded, in this conception, as major virtues.

3. One of the most vivid examples of the enormous disparity among the resources schools have available is found in Kozol (1991).

4. The achievement of parity between university professors and those who work in elementary, middle, and secondary schools is not likely to occur unless increased discretionary time is made available for teachers and school administrators and unless the reward system for promotion in higher education acknowledges the contributions that are made to the practice of education by being engaged in schools with educational practitioners. At the most sophisticated research universities, such recognition has yet to come when appraisals are made regarding matters of promotion and retention.

5. Not included in the dimensions I have just identified are university admissions criteria, the Scholastic Aptitude Test, the Advanced Placement Tests, and community expectations. All of the foregoing are critical dimensions for effective school reform.

Chapter 2

1. For a treatment of cognition as essentially dealing with thought mediated by language, see, for example, Anderson (1975).

2. Jean Piaget (1973) notes that "the affective and cognitive mechanism always remain indissociable although distinct" (p. 47).

3. Rudolf Arnheim (1969) notes that in early Greek philosophy, "Sensory perception and reasoning were established as antagonists, in need of each other but different from each other in principle. . . . The mistrust of ordinary perception marks Plato's philosophy profoundly" (pp. 6, 8).

4. In behaviorism the term has a central place, i.e., stimulus–response. This pair of terms was at the core of the theory developed by one of America's most influential educational psychologists, E. L. Thorndike.

5. Indeed, it is important to distinguish between behavior and action. For an excellent commentary on this distinction, see Green (1971).

6. Watson (1914) argued against introspection in psychology: "One must believe that two hundred years from now, unless the introspection method is discarded, psychology will still be divided on the question as to whether auditory sensations have the quality of 'extension,' whether intensity is an attribute which can be applied to color, whether there is a difference in 'texture' between image and sensation; and upon many hundreds of others of like character. . . . The time seems to have come when psychology must discard all reference to consciousness" (p. 8).

7. Herbert Read (1945) writes on the contribution of art to consciousness: "What is now suggested, in opposition to the whole of the logico-rationalistic tradition, is that there exists a concrete visual mode of 'thinking,' a mental process which reaches its highest efficiency in the work of art. It is a mode of thinking which sustains that primary unity of perception and feeling found in the eidetic disposition. This primary unity develops into the unity of sensibility and reason (sensation and ideas) and is then the basis of all imaginative and practical activity" (p. 69).

8. The style and content of professional journals perform an extremely important socializing function in a field of study since access to journals affects the young scholar's view of what is competent and influences his or her chances for publication and promotion.

9. For the educational utility of graphic aids, see, for example, Barrich (1972), Birkimer & Brown (1979), Effing (1977), and Feshbach et al. (1978). For a discussion of the special capacities of holography, see Ouosh (1976).

Chapter 3

1. The notion "competent eye" refers to the fact that perception is both cognitive and transactional. Seeing is an achievement dependent upon visual literacy.

2. Images may be regarded as the generic process of creating mental

structures through which the world is comprehended in the sciences as well as in the arts.

3. No single form of representation can reveal all that can be experienced; hence, representation, like perception, is selective.

4. Habituation to particular forms of representation tends to increase both the skills and satisfactions secured from using them.

5. I am indebted to Rudolf Arnheim for this observation.

6. Aristotle writes in *Ethics,* "as Agathon says, 'Art loves chance and chance loves art.' Art, then, as has been said, is a state concerned with making, involving a true course of reasoning, and a lack of art on the contrary is a state concerned with making, involving a false course of reasoning; both are concerned with the variable" (p. 116).

7. See, for example, Bellack (1966), Bowers & Flinders (1990), and Flanders (1970).

8. Exemplification is used not only in teaching children, but also in the making of science. Model making is the effort to exemplify relationships.

9. Aristotle *(Ethics)* distinguishes between the deliberative, which is rationality applied to the variable, and the calculative, which is applied to the invariable and is "one part of the faculty which grasps a rational principle" (p. 114). Deliberation is associated with practical wisdom, or "correctness of thinking . . . [while] searching for something and calculating" (p. 122).

Chapter 4

1. It seems interesting to note that the current press toward clarity of aim and outcome and the effort to systematize the relationship among goals, standards, assessment, and curriculum is a way of reducing ambiguity, as if ambiguity were alien to intellectual processes. Technicist approaches to school improvement are likely to eviscerate the very spirit that schools most desperately need, a spirit that encourages the exercise of imagination and the pursuit of those tasks beyond immediate reach.

2. Schools serving upper-middle-class communities, in particular, are often pressed by parents to push down the content of the first and second grade into the kindergarten. It strikes me that just the reverse would be in order: the best features of the kindergarten should be extended into the first and second grades.

3. Stanford, for example, does not include grades in the fine arts when it calculates the grade-point average of high school seniors seeking admission. Ironically, Stanford awards degrees in the very fields for which it denies high school students acknowledgment of their performance.

4. The School of Education at Stanford has made heroic and I believe successful efforts to establish close links between the School of Education and schools in the Bay Area of California. These links aspire to a sense of parity rather than simply regarding schools as resources for the conduct of professorially driven educational research.

5. Recent efforts at what is called "authentic assessment" often encourage students and teachers to collect work samples in order to construct a portfolio. An essential problem in portfolios is not the collection of work samples, but the development of criteria useful for knowing how to assess what is in the portfolio. This requires not only conceptual sophistication but also levels of connoisseurship that will make it possible for judges, whether students or teachers, to fairly appraise the quality of the work the portfolio contains. This will be a labor-intensive activity. Whether school districts will be willing to provide the time necessary for this kind of assessment to go forward remains to be seen. Optical scanners, though considerably more efficient, are insensitive to the very qualities that authentic assessment can reveal.

References

Anderson, B. F. (1975). *Cognitive psychology*. New York: Academic Press.

Aristotle. (1973). *Ethics*. (J. L. Ackrill, Ed.). London: Faber & Faber.

Arnheim, R. (1954). *Art and visual perception*. Berkeley: University of California Press.

Arnheim, R. (1969). *Visual thinking*. Berkeley: University of California Press.

Ayer, A. (n.d.). *Language, truth, and logic*. New York: Dover.

Barker, R. (1968). *Ecological psychology*. Stanford, CA: Stanford University Press.

Barrich, M. P. (1972). Log-log plotting as a tool in high school physics. *Physics Teacher, 10*, 37–39.

Bellack, A. A. (1966). *Language of the classroom*. New York: Teachers College Press.

Berman, Weiler Associates. (1988). *Restructuring California education: A design for public education in the twenty-first century* (Recommendations to the California Business Roundtable). Berkeley, CA: Author.

Bernstein, B. (1971). On the classification and framing of educational knowledge. In M. Young (Ed.), *Knowledge and control* (pp. 47–69). London: Collier, Macmillan.

Birkimer, J. C., & Brown, J. H. (1979). Graphical judgmental aid which summarizes obtained and chance reliability data and helps assess the believability of experimental effects. *Journal of Applied Behavorial Analysis, 12*, 523–533.

Bowers, C. A., & Flinders, D. J. (1990). *Responsive teaching: An ecological approach to classroom patterns of language, culture, and thought*. New York: Teachers College Press.

Broudy, H., Smith, B., & Burnett, J. (1964). *Democracy and excellence in American secondary education*. Chicago: Rand McNally.

Bruner, J. (1961). *The process of education*. Cambridge, MA: Harvard University Press.

Bruner, J. (1971). *The relevance of education*. New York: Norton.

Bruner, J. (1990). *Acts of meaning*. Cambridge, MA: Harvard University Press.

California State Board of Education. (1987). *History–social sciences framework for California public schools*. Sacramento: California State Department of Education.

Chomsky, N. (1973). Foreword. In A. Schaff, *Language and cognition* (R. Cohen, Ed.). New York: McGraw-Hill.

Cohen, E. (1986). *Designing group work: Strategies for the heterogeneous classroom*. New York: Teachers College Press.

Cole, M. (1974). *Culture and thought: A psychological introduction*. New York: Wiley.

College Entrance Examination Board. (1989). *National report on college-bound seniors, 1989*. New York: Author.

Collingwood, R. (1958). *The principles of art*. New York: Oxford University Press.

Descartes, R. (1992). *Meditations on first philosophy*. Notre Dame: University of Notre Dame Press.

Dewey, J. (1938). *Experience and education*. New York: Macmillan.

Dewey, J. (1958). *Art as experience*. New York: Putnam. (Original work published 1934)

Dissanyake, E. (1991). *Art for life's sake*. Washington, DC: National Art Education Association.

Downey, L. (1960). *The task of public education*. Chicago: University of Chicago Press.

Dreeben, R. (1968). *On what is learned in school*. New York: Addison-Wesley.

Effing, M. (1977). Prepresenting image formation in lenses and mirrors. *Physics Teacher, 15*, 178–179.

Eisner, E. W. (1985). *The educational imagination: On the design and evaluation of education programs* (2nd ed.). New York: Macmillan.

Eisner, E. W. (1991a). Curriculum ideologies. In P. Jackson (Ed.), *Handbook of research on curriculum* (pp. 302–326). New York: Macmillan.

Eisner, E. (1991b). *The enlightened eye: Qualitative inquiry and the enhancement of educational practice*. New York: Macmillan.

Epstein, T. (1989). *An aesthetic approach to the teaching and learning of the social studies*. Doctoral dissertation, Harvard University, Cambridge, MA.

Epstein, T. (in press). Sometimes a shining moment: High school students' creations of the arts in historical contexts. *Social Education*.

Feshbach, N. A., et al. (1978). Demonstration of the use of graphics in teaching children nutrition. *Journal of Nutrition Education, 10*, 124–126.

Finn, C. (1991). *We must take charge*. New York: Maxwell Macmillan International.

Flanders, N. A. (1970). *Analyzing teaching behavior*. Reading, MA: Addison-Wesley.

Gardner, H. (1973). *The arts and human development*. New York: Wiley.

Gardner, H. (1983). *Frames of mind*. New York: Basic Books.

Gazzaniga, M., & Sperry, R. (1967). Language after section of the cerebral commissures. *Brain, 90*(1), 131–248.

Gibbon, E. (1963). *Decline and fall of the Roman empire*. New York: Twayne. (Original work published 1788)

Giroux, H. (1989). *Critical pedagogy, the state, and cultural struggle*. Albany: State University of New York Press.

Gombrich, E. (1969). Visual discovery through art. In J. Hogg (Ed.), *Psychology and the visual arts* (pp. 215–238). Middlesex, England: Penguin.

Goodman, N. (1968). *Languages of art*. Indianapolis: Bobbs-Merrill.

Gregory, R. (1966). *Eye and brain*. New York: McGraw-Hill.

Green, T. (1971). *Activities of teaching*. New York: McGraw-Hill.

Greeno, J. (1989). Perspectives on thinking. *American Psychologist, 44*(2), 134–141.

Hadamard, J. (1949). *An essay on the psychology of invention in the mathematical field*. Princeton, NJ: Princeton University Press.

Health Education Council. (1980, January 24). Winter Warmth, Sudbury, Suffolk, England. *The Guardian*, p. 5.

Holton, G. (1967–1968). Influences on Einstein's early work in relativity theory. *American Scholar, 37*, 959–979.

Jackson, P. (1986). *The practice of teaching*. New York: Teachers College Press.

James, W. (1890). *The principles of psychology* (Vol. 1). New York: Henry Holt.

Kilpatrick, W. (1919). *The project method*. New York: Teachers College.

Koestler, A. (1949). *Insight and outlook*. New York: Macmillan.

Kohl, H. (1969). *The open classroom*. New York: New York Review.

Kozol, J. (1991). *Savage inequalities*. New York: Crown.

Kuffler, S., & Nicolls, J. (1976). *From neuron to brain: A cellular approach to the function of the neuron systems*. Sunderland, MA: Sinovar Associates.

Langer, S. (1942). *Philosophy in a new key*. Cambridge, MA: Harvard University Press.

Langer, S. (1957). *Problems of art*. New York: Charles Scribners Sons.

McNeill, W. (1963). *The rise of the West*. Chicago: University of Chicago Press.

National Commission on Excellence in Education. (1983). *A nation at risk*. Washington, DC: U.S. Government Printing Office.

Neisser, U. (1976). *Cognition and reality: Principles and implications of cognitive psychology*. San Francisco: Freeman.

Olson, D. (1978, October 26–28). The arts and education: Three cognitive functions of symbols. Paper presented at the Terman Memorial Conference, Stanford, CA.

Ouosh, T. (1976). *Three-dimensional imaging techniques*. New York: Academic Press.

Oxford English dictionary. (1961). Oxford, UK: Clarendon.

Piaget, J. (1973). *The child and reality*. New York: Grossman.

Piaget, J. (1977). *The development of thought: Equilibration of cognitive structures*. New York: Viking Press.

Plato (1951). *The republic* (F. Cornford, Tr.). New York: Oxford University Press.

Popper, K. (1945). *The open society and its enemies.* London: Routledge & Kegan Paul.

Pylyshyn, Z. W. (1986). *Computation and cognition: Toward a foundation for cognitive science.* Cambridge, MA: MIT Press.

Read, H. (1945). *Education through art.* New York: Pantheon.

Rosenberg, H. (1965). *American painting today.* New York: Horizon Press.

Saloman, G. (1979). *Interaction of media cognition, and learning.* San Francisco: Jossey-Bass.

Sarason, S. (1990). *The predictable failure of educational reform.* San Francisco: Jossey-Bass.

Schaff, A. (1973). *Language and cognition* (R. Cohen, Ed.). New York: McGraw-Hill.

Shepard, R. (1982). *Mental images and their transformation.* Cambridge, MA: MIT Press.

Shirer, W. (1960). *Rise and fall of the Third Reich.* New York: Simon & Schuster.

Singer, M. (1991). *Sound, image, and word in the curriculum: The making of historical sense.* Doctoral dissertation, Stanford University, Stanford, CA.

Singer-Gabella, M. (1992). *Beyond the looking glass: Bringing students into the conversation of historical inquiry.* Unpublished manuscript, Vanderbilt University, Nashville, TN.

Singer-Gabella, M. (1993, April). *Textual truths, photographic facts: Epistemological stumbling blocks in the study of history.* Paper presented at annual meeting of the American Educational Research Association, Atlanta.

Stanford University (1990). *Looking ahead to Stanford.* [Undergraduate application material].

Thucydides. (1972). *History of the Pelopennesian War.* Baltimore, MD: Penguin Books.

Toynbee, A. (1953). *The world and the West.* New York: Oxford University Press.

Tuchman, B. (1962). *The guns of August.* New York: Macmillan.

Uhrmacher, B. (1991). *Waldorf schools marching quietly unheard.* Doctoral Dissertation, Stanford University, Stanford, CA.

U.S. Department of Education. (1987). *What works: Research about teaching and learning* (2nd ed.). Washington, DC: Author.

U.S. Department of Education. (1991). *America 2000.* No. 1. (Week of September 1, 1991). Washington, DC.

Watson, J. B. (1914). *Behavior: An introduction to comparative psychology.* New York: Henry Holt.

White, B. (1971). *Human infants: Experience and psychological development.* Englewood Cliffs, NJ: Prentice-Hall.

Index

About the Author

Elliot Eisner is Professor of Education and Art at Stanford University. He has served as President of the American Educational Research Association, the National Art Education Association, and the International Society for Education through Art. His books include *The Educational Imagination* (3rd ed.; Macmillan, 1994), *The Enlightened Eye* (Macmillan, 1991), and, with Alan Peshkin, *Qualitative Inquiry: The Continuing Debate* (Teachers College Press, 1990).